THE UNDERDOG
CHURCH-PLANTER

the
underdog
church-planter

being a 1-star planter in a 5-star world

Contributors:

Steve Anderson

Al Barrera

Dan Freng

Mark Hallock

Kevin Hasenack

Jeff Jung

Jim Misloski

Fabian Perea

Evan Skelton

Matt Whitt

General Editors:

Jenna Hallock, Mark Hallock, & Evan Skelton

ACOMA PRESS

contents

acknowledgments

We want to thank each of our wonderful, Calvary Church congregations. What a joy it is to serve you as together we seek to make Jesus non-ignorable.

Thanks to each of our wives and children who have supported us, not simply in this writing process, but through our shared mission to make Jesus famous to the glory of God through church planting.

Special thanks to Jenna Hallock for helping us to edit these chapters and make them better than they ever could have been on their own.

Finally, all thanks and praise be to the God who chooses to use all types of underdogs for His purposes in and through local churches all over the world. *Soli Deo Gloria.*

contributors

Steve Anderson serves as an Associate Pastor at Calvary Englewood in Englewood, Colorado. Originally from the East Coast, Steve headed west to Colorado to attend seminary and has now served in ministry here for over 10 years. Steve earned his BS from Gordon College and his MDiv from Denver Seminary. Steve's main ministry is to his wife Sarah, and their sons, Wadely and William.

Al Barrera is a Colorado Native, called out from a career as a Journeyman Electrician, and has since worked in Ministry Leadership as a college pastor, young adults minister, revitalizing senior pastor, a church-planter, and now as a Church Planting Catalyst for the North American Mission Board. A graduate of Golden Gate Baptist Theological Seminary, Al is currently pursuing his Doctorate of Ministry with Gateway Seminary. He and his wife of over 15 years, Marcy, live with their four beautiful daughters in Parker, CO, a suburb of Denver. He is a serving member of Calvary Church, Denver, loving people in the heart of one of the most diverse areas of the city.

Dan Freng serves as the Lead Pastor at Calvary Church Littleton in Littleton, Colorado. Dan earned his BA from Southwest Minnesota State University and his MDiv from Denver Seminary. Dan's main ministry is to his wife, Kelly, and their kids Noah, Jasmine, Isaac, Brian, and Shamie. Dan's passion is reaching out to people in the community and connecting them to the local church.

Mark Hallock serves as the Lead Pastor of Calvary Church Englewood in Englewood, Colorado and as a National Replanting Catalyst with the North American Mission Board. He is grateful for 17 years of marriage to his wife, Jenna, and loves being a daddy to their kids, Zoe and Eli. He earned his MDiv from Denver Seminary and his Doctor of Ministry from Westminster Theological Seminary.

Kevin Hasenack serves as the Lead Pastor of Calvary Church Denver. He earned his BA from New Mexico State University and his MTS from Golden Gate Baptist Theological Seminary. Kevin loves his wife, Jenn and his sweet daughter Charlie. He loves doing intercultural ministry and connecting those that are far from Jesus to the Savior!

Jeff Jung serves as the Lead Pastor of Calvary Church Aurora. He was born in S. Korea, but grew up in Reno, NV. After high school, he attended the University of Nevada Reno where he earned a degree in music, and more importantly, met his wife, Jihyun. After getting married in 2005, they moved to Mill Valley, CA to study at Golden Gate Baptist Theological Seminary where he earned his M.Div. Jeff and Jihyun thank the Lord for their four beautiful children.

Jim Misloski serves as the State Director of Missions for the Colorado Baptist Convention and a pastor at Calvary Church Englewood in Englewood, Colorado. He enjoys spending time in God's beautiful creation with his wife Paula and three children Perry, Ellen and Davis.

Fabian Perea serves as the Lead Pastor of Calvary en Español. Fabian is from Venezuela and has been married to his wife, Marianela, for 25 years. They have two beautiful children, Fabian Rafael and Ana Karina. Fabian has been in the ministry for more than 27 years. He has helped plant 14 churches in Venezuela and is now planting the 15th: Calvary en Español in Englewood, Colorado. His studies include a Bachelor in Theology from the Venezuelan Baptist Theological Seminary. His great passion is to develop leaders who can take the Gospel to the unreached through the planting of new churches.

Evan Skelton serves as a pastor at Calvary Church Denver and has lived in sight of the Denver skyline for most of his life. He earned his BA in Pastoral Ministry from Moody Bible Institute and his MDiv from Denver Seminary. Evan and his wife, Grace, are loving the adventure of raising Clara and Oliver, and Evan looks forward to shepherding his family and the church for years to come, hopefully over a root beer and a Chipotle burrito.

Matt Whitt serves as the Lead Pastor of Calvary Church La Junta in La Junta, Colorado. After serving as a Calvary and NAMB replanting intern, Matt and his wife and their two kids moved to La Junta, a small plains town in south eastern Colorado, to replant a church that was set to close its doors. Matt earned his BA from Eastern University and his MDiv from Denver Seminary.

foreword

God is at work in our city. We have been praying and are now beginning to see a special wave and move of God that is emerging and spreading in our city and along the Front Range. This movement has humble beginnings and very ignorable paths. Several years ago, a church that was struggling to stay alive decided to take one more chance by trying another pastor. This church was in an "Underdog" situation, but this pastor was unique. He began as an "underdog" himself with a solid theological integrity, a heart of a visionary shepherd, a love for people, and a joyful attitude that has become contagious.

Pastor Mark Hallock has been used of God to draw a band of brothers together to advance the gospel and make Jesus non-ignorable in the city of Denver and along the Front Range. Lodged in the heart of this man of God is a desire not only revitalize existing churches and replant dying churches, but a desire to plant new churches. His passion has energized others to come alongside and help prepare God-called men into gospel driven work in the trenches of church ministry and church planting.

Gospel ministry is a high calling, but it is hard work as well. It requires mastering some "basic" core competencies in order to equip workers in church planting.

This resource is written for the underdogs who know no better than to depend on God, obey his calling, and make Jesus non-ignorable by sharing and living out the gospel along the Front Range.

I recommend you take this resource which provides the basics of ministry to heart and apply these basic core principles into your lifestyle, until these healthy habits become the core competencies of your ministry.

Approach this resource in a humble fashion, since this story has humble beginnings. You can become part of this movement if you approach it with the same spirit of humility and joy. For, if you do and learn and live out the principles by God's grace, this movement will occur within you, and God will use you to spread it along the Front Range, flooding this city and the West.

Dave Howeth
Send City Missionary - Denver
North American Mission Board

PART 1

foundations
for the underdog church-planter

CHAPTER 1

God loves underdogs... and He always has

Al Barrera

"You're 5 foot nothin', 100 and nothin', and you have barely a speck of athletic ability. And you hung in there with the best college football players in the land for two years. And you're gonna walk outta here with a degree from the University of Notre Dame. In this life, you don't have to prove nothin' to nobody but yourself. And after what you've gone through, if you haven't done that by now, it ain't gonna never happen."

- Rudy, 1993

I have to say, that quote gets me every time!! For those who do not recognize it, that line is from the movie *Rudy*...one of those impossible stories that screams "Hollywood!!!!" but is actually based on real events and real people. For fans of sports movies, like myself, the quote is iconic and stands as one of the most memorable in the inspirational, sports-movie genre. But to truly "get it" you have to picture the scene: the mentor/coach, standing at the end of a darkened corridor with his willing student, is growing tired of listening to the emotional whining of a young guy at the end of his rope. Sure, the kid's made it to places he never should have, college itself being one of them, but within the context of the story, playing football at Notre Dame had remained Rudy's ultimate goal. He pursued it with a passionate focus, pushing everything aside to reach this self-defined pinnacle of existence. He needed to play in just one game to be counted, in the books, as being a Notre Dame football player. As a second string player, he'd given all he had, in order to possibly "suit up" for one real game and run through that tunnel onto the field. No one believed that would ever happen. I mean, everyone had told Rudy that he couldn't play...his teachers and coaches, his former fiancé, his brothers, even his father. People had been telling Rudy his whole life he wasn't good enough: "You're too small…you're too average. You're not smart enough…strong enough…talented enough." "Just work in the factory, marry the girl next door, and settle." But Rudy couldn't do that. Instead, he pursued his dreams…heading off on a journey he alone believed he could achieve, praying that reality could some day match his drive and desire. He alone knew and believed that someday he'd prove they were all wrong. He'd prove that he was special. He'd prove that he had what it takes!

So here they stand, mentor and student, at the end of the dark tunnel leading out into the bright light of the stadium. Recessed in the shadows, Rudy cries about all he's been denied (after all he'd been through, he wasn't going to get the chance to "dress")…searching for an ally, he tells his mentor that he can't go on, not even for one more practice. Rudy doesn't see the light…he doesn't see the wide-open spaces of the field ahead of him…he simply dwells in the dark tunnel of a situation he has faced before; a closed door that doesn't seem like an opportunity as much as one more battle to fight. He's tired. So his mentor's voice firmly interrupts and reminds him of the challenges he's already faced, of the victories he's already won. As all good mentors do, he reminds him of the ultimate goal. And Rudy, the unlikely warrior, steps up one more time.

That's the underdog story. In the face of reality, it's the desperate idea that more is possible. Think about it…how many films, books, songs, stories, and poems have been written with this idea in mind? Throughout human history, this underdog appreciation has captivated readers, listeners, and viewers. Why? Why does their story so inspire the masses? Why do people line up to watch *Rocky Balboa* get pummeled only to keep coming back? To watch Vince Papale stand *Invincible*, embracing his shot at playing for the Philadelphia Eagles, while personally doubting his own abilities, his own worth, and whether or not he can take one more hit? The list goes on and on, right? *Hoosiers, Cinderella Man, The Karate Kid, Moneyball, Miracle,* even *Finding Nemo*…each tale drawing us in with the impossibility of the task and begging us to believe. But it doesn't end with movies: Steinbeck's Lenny in *Of Mice and Men*, Tolkien's Frodo Baggins in the *Lord of the Ring* Series, S.E. Hinton's Ponyboy in *The Outsiders*, Rowling's *Harry Potter* Series. We are obsessed with underdogs! We stoically rise, slow-clapping with the characters, yelling at the top of our lungs, "We believe! We believe! We believe!" And in our hearts we do, like children clapping for Tinker Bell and her fairy companions. We do believe that the impossible can happen and that maybe, just maybe, the fairytale could be true. What is it about these stories that capture our hearts and minds?

The Underdog Life

As I think about my own reactions to stories like these, I have to say, what draws me into the "what if's" of underdog tales are not necessarily the ways in which the underdogs achieve victory in the end. *Friday Night Lights* didn't end well for the tough, little team from Odessa, Texas, yet the story remains one of my absolute favorites. If I'm honest, I think what draws me into the mythic underdog tale is the failure. I identify with things not working out like planned...the reality of trying and not succeeding. That's me...that's us...that's the human experience!

Thinking about my life, there have been far more "crushed dreams" than "full-on successes", and as human beings, we share that connection. Failure binds people together. In the realness of pain and heartbreak, failure makes heroes spring to life in ways that stories of flawless victory never can. It's in the loss that we connect, brushing away blurry-eyed tears of remembrance. We recall our battles, standing like David in front of Goliath and remember when the stone we cast at the giant's head missed by inches. We root for the underdog, dreaming he achieves what we couldn't. But we know in the back of our minds that even if victory eludes, hope still exists in the midst of the pain that will follow. Underdog stories remind us of the frailty of our dreams and the reality that even when things don't turn out like we planned, we can still continue to dream. Underdog tales are total life-stories wrapped up in a situational context. They're systematic tales that illustrate the totality of life bound in a focused play of win or lose, victory or defeat. Think about the general formula of the underdog tale:

1. Life being lived but not to a full potential...Dreams of something more
2. Detractors from the Dream
3. Attempts to Make Dreams Reality
4. **Opposition**

   (Repeat Cycle Until...)

5. **Moment of Change**
6. Small Victory
7. Encouraging Voice

8. Larger Victory
9. Encouraging Voice
10. Final Attempt at the Impossible Victory
11. Encouraging Voice
12. **Failure or Success???**

When we think about that formula, we see a pattern emerge. We see the dreamer, the underdog, in the story who sees the capacity within, the need for change, but doesn't know what to do to change the circumstances of life. We see a pattern of detractors...those voices who either want to see the main character stay in a place of misery and dissatisfaction or just can't see the talents hidden beneath the surface of the main protagonist's character. We see attempts and failure, a repeated pattern of setbacks to the goal, and through each, the detractors announce more and more loudly, "I TOLD YOU SO! Stop trying, stop fighting, resign yourself to the reality of your situation."

Then, we see an opportunity...one catalyzing moment that projects the main character's activity to a place where he or she asks, "Is this my chance? Is this what I've been waiting for?" And in a moment of faith, the main character steps out...moving forward...and the voices of the detractors start to increasingly dim. Not because they see the opportunity for what it is, but because in that moment, the voices of "reason" become less important than the hopes and dreams of the unlikely hero in the tale. Sometimes the skeptical voices are within the main character...because at times in life, self-doubts ring the loudest.

Doggedly the hero pushes through, shoving doubt aside, and suddenly there's a small victory. And in that victory other voices begin to emerge. They may have been present throughout the story, but rapidly those voices of encouragement begin to grow louder than those saying, "You can't!"

Soon after, another message is whispered and heard, "Maybe you can?" All of this leads, throughout victories and set-backs, to an ultimate finale in which the main character faces one final battle, one concluding moment that will prove, once and for all, whether the struggle, the fight, was worth it.

The most interesting thing about the underdog tale is the variety of ways in which final "victory" is achieved. It's not always found in the "win or lose" category. Sometimes the drama is not even captured in the contest at hand, the reason for the tale. Sometimes we see victory happen without even caring about a final vote or a final score. Who watched the end of the first *Rocky* movie and actually cared about whether Rocky beat Apollo Creed or not? Instead, we waited, on the edge of our seats, to see if Adrian made it through the crowd to tell Rocky she loved him.

The movie wasn't great because he won (spoiler alert—Rocky lost the first fight); the movie was great because Rocky "won" what was most important. He won because even though he was filled with self-doubt about his pugilistic capabilities, he never quit, and he fought *THE BIG FIGHT*. He won because love became more important to him than proving he deserved to fight at all. Throughout the course of the film, we saw Rocky move from isolated loner, focused on the chances he never got, to a man surrounded by people who truly cared about him. And we saw him care right back! We saw him move past anger and fear and transform into a man who, even though filled with the ghosts of his past, was willing to continue to dream that he was worth loving…that he was worth supporting…that he was worth fighting for!

We saw Rocky become part of something more, and we ached to be part of something more ourselves. The fight in *Rocky* wasn't about boxing…it was about rejoining humanity and about loving and being loved. We recognized the *Rocky* in us, and although few of us will ever fight for the World Title in boxing, we recognize that every day we have the choice to fight…every day we make a decision either to keep moving forward and to keep dreaming or to step back and withdraw, dwelling in the lonely land of regret and blame. Through stories like *Rocky*, we learn punch-by-punch that failure is not simply facing opposition; failure is facing opposition and then giving up on our hopes for the future and choosing to quit.

What About the "Winners"?

So why do we so identify with the underdogs in these stories? What about those talent-filled individuals that these underdogs often face? Why don't we stand up in the middle of *Cinderella Man* and scream, "Go Max Baer!!! Beat Jim Braddock!!!" Why can't I root for Drago in *Rocky IV*? For Voldemort in *Harry Potter*? Okay, well maybe that's going a little too far… unless I'm also happily cheering for the Emperor in *Return of the Jedi*, Biff in *Back to the Future* ("McFly???"), and *Jaws* the shark seeking out his buffet of senseless swimmers and ornery sea captains. But really, why don't we root for the winners? Think about it. Isn't that exactly what we want for the underdogs? To become winners? Don't we want them to have a chance to stand in the spotlight and receive the accolades? To be cheered by the masses and to be recognized for being the best?

Malcolm Gladwell, in his book *David and Goliath: Underdogs, Misfits, and The Art of Battling Giants*, has several theories regarding the societal draw towards the underdog narrative. Early in his book he makes this statement: "What we consider valuable in our world arises out of these kinds of lopsided conflicts (underdog tales), because the act of facing overwhelming odds produces greatness and beauty."[1] He goes on to say something profound, "The fact of being the underdog can *change* people in ways we often fail to appreciate: it can open doors and create opportunities and educate and enlighten and make possible what might otherwise have seemed unthinkable."[2] Think about that statement…just *being* the underdog, just *being* in the position of facing ridiculous odds, can cause such transformation <u>in</u> the individual (not to mention those observing the challenge being faced) to bring about a radical shift in the trajectory of a life.

Perhaps this is what lies beneath the fascination we have with the underdog narrative. Could it all come back to the idea that we long for a transformed existence and therefore, vicariously, we attempt to impact the trajectory of our lives through the "wins" of the underdogs in the stories we cheer? I think this might be the case. That although we long for the underdog to "make it", we identify more with the struggle to get there than the actual arrival. The victory is in the journey. And although we long from afar to be connected to the "winners", we identify most with the underdogs…those guys who through failure have learned the hard lessons that have led to the important changes taking place.

This isn't a far cry from the ideas set forth by the author of the book of Hebrews in the New Testament. In discussing the perseverance of God in regard to salvation and the deliverance of His people, the author encourages Followers of Jesus to persevere and continue moving forward in the hope of what will be:

> God is not unjust; he will not forget your work and the love you have shown him as you have helped his people and continue to help them. We want each of you to show this same diligence to the very end, so that what you hope for may be fully realized.[3]

It's not about what currently "is"…it's about striving forward into full assurance of the hopes and dreams of what "might be". It's not the assumption that an individual is good enough, smart enough, capable enough, or even talented enough; it's about acknowledging the fact that, in and of themselves, they are none of these things. Only through the work of God can anything of worth be accomplished. It's about effectively mimicking the resolution of the Author of all good things and realizing that in the journey there will be tears and pain and difficulty, but *perseverance will build a character worth having.*

It comes back to the difficulty of the journey again, doesn't it? This reminds me of a test called the CRT or Cognitive Reflection Test. This test makes up what some refer to as "the world's shortest intelligence test". [4] The findings of this test, after giving it to some of the brainiest college students around, were surprising. Although no one (not even the smartest students) were able to perfectly pass the test, the test developers discovered the way to improve test scores was to make the test even harder. Testers changed font size, changed colors of font, and the results were that test scores went up…dramatically! It was in the hard work of squinting and deciphering that test-takers had to process the information in a different way, and the difficulty level forced them to truly earn the scores. This takes us back to Gladwell's quote from earlier: "the act of facing overwhelming odds produces greatness and beauty." In striving, there is beauty found. In the heartache, the character is made. In observing the struggle, the fan of the underdog is lifted up and encouraged to keep moving forward.

Cortland Myers, in the devotional masterpiece *Streams in the Desert,* describes this character-building process, after first describing the additive development of steel being formed with iron *plus* fire, soil developing by rock *plus* heat *plus* pressure: "The development of human character requires a 'plus' attached to it, for great character is not made through luxurious living but through suffering. And the world does not forget people of great character." [5] The winners are impressive but it's the struggle of the underdog, of the unqualified, of the undeserving, with which we most identify. It's in that struggle, and the beautiful results that ensue, that cause us all to stand and scream, "I can relate! I can overcome! I can go on!!" The simple truth is we want our underdogs to win, but we want them to earn those wins. Like us, we want them to taste failure so that in the humility of defeat they can rise up and keep moving forward…they can become great and unforgettable. We don't root for Apollo Creed because we haven't personified his greatness, and we haven't experienced his failure. His win hasn't become our win. His taste of failure isn't our taste. Winning without experiencing the humility of failure is characterless and lacking, and we struggle to relate.

God's Heart for the Underdog

Perhaps these ideas of failure and humility, being unimpressive, under-qualified, and undeserving are the reason why God, throughout time, has chosen to use these types of people to accomplish amazing tasks. Browse the pages of Scripture and again and again we see that God has utilized the underdog to accomplish great things. Everyone God has ever used has carried some type of flaw, some type of difficulty, or at the very least some type of perceived flaw. Walk through the names: Abraham—gave into his fear and consistently struggled with patience issues; Isaac—dealt poorly with conflict and favored one son over another; Jacob—wrestled with cowardice as a manipulative momma's boy; Moses—struck out in angry frustration, almost forfeiting his calling to lead God's people, because of fear-driven speech issues. How about the story of David? We're familiar with the catalyst for his popularity (his famous battle with the giant, Goliath), but what about before that? Where was David? He was the youngest son of Jesse of Bethlehem, sitting out in the pastures, faithfully guarding sheep. He was a lowly shepherd. He was small. He was insignificant. He was disregarded.

In the story from 1 Samuel 16, the Lord told the prophet Samuel to travel to Bethlehem to anoint one of the sons of Jesse to the role of King of Israel. One of the sons of Jesse would become "the man" to replace the current wayward king, Saul. So Samuel obeyed the command of God, took the trip, and Jesse presented the most impressive of his sons. In fact, as Jesse ran through seven of his sons, no doubt in order of impressive attributes (the oldest, the best warriors, the most obvious choices for King), Samuel finally asked, "Are these all the sons you have?" Samuel's seen the best. He's seen the most qualified…the ones with the credentials. He's seen the candidates most fully supported by their father as men who could be successful in the role of King of Israel. "Are these all the sons you have?" "There is still the youngest," Jesse answered, "but he is tending the sheep." *There's still one more Sam…but really. David? Our little shepherd boy? He's unimpressive…he's no leader of people. He can help you get the herd across a creek but guide a people?? Not David.* Samuel responded,

"Send for him…" "So (Jesse) sent and had him brought in. He was ruddy, with a fine appearance and handsome features. Then the Lord said, 'Rise and anoint him. He is the one'"(1 Sam. 16:12).

Can you imagine the reaction of Jesse? Of the brothers? This boy being anointed, with all of his deficiencies…how could this be?? It goes back to what the Lord told Samuel earlier in the chapter: "The Lord does not look at the things man looks at. Man looks at the outward appearance, but the Lord looks at the heart." In this story, the Lord revealed His "fundamental otherness", His foundational ability to make the humbled lowly into unexpected heroes, in his use of humanity to accomplish His concerns; the beauty of this passage is that it draws incredible distinction between man's judge of potential success and the human capacity to overcome insufficiencies through God's mighty hand of guidance and supremacy.[6] God is not limited in what He can accomplish through the most qualified or unqualified candidates. *He* is fully capable; therefore anyone He chooses to use, whether deemed qualified, talented, or appropriate by others, can be empowered to accomplish great things.

Another biblical example can be seen in the life of none other than Jesus Christ. Now albeit, He is not the model underdog (100% man, 100% God, 100% of the time); but if looked at again, from an outside appearance, there is nothing that qualified Jesus, as God Incarnate, for the role of redeemer of the world. In forecasting the prophesy of the coming Messiah, Isaiah described him in this way:

> He grew up before him like a tender shoot,
>   and like a root out of dry ground.
> He had no beauty or majesty to attract us to him,
>   nothing in his appearance that we should desire him. (Is.53:2)

Jesus didn't possess anything from an outside physical manifestation that announced His worth. Nothing physically drew people to Him. From a social standpoint, Jesus had many things working against him, starting from His birth: He was the illegitimate son of an unwed mother, the undesirable inhabitant of a disregarded place called Nazareth. His followers later in life were not much better: dirty and uneducated fishermen; tax collectors and sinners; women. He died a death that held nothing but scorn and rejection, taking on a cultural curse in its very practice: "Christ redeemed us from the curse of the law by becoming a curse for us, for it is written: 'Cursed is everyone who is hung on a pole'" (Gal.3:13).

But Jesus, as the ultimate underdog story, didn't whither into oblivion based on his suffering or pain or neglect or even His death. Instead, like the underdog tales of *Rudy* and *Rocky* and *The Outsiders*, Jesus came back! He returned from defeat, travelling forward from oblivion, to pronounce to the world, in all His Majesty, that He had conquered death and sin. He trumpeted from a platform of Sovereign rule that no longer would humanity exist in a place of uncertainty and separation. Instead, humanity would be lifted up, in the most unique vicarious victory of all time, to a place of relationship with the God of All Creation, through His underdog victory over all that would condemn and destroy and distract.

> In all these things we are more than conquerors through Him who loved us. For I am convinced that neither death nor life, neither angels nor demons, neither the present nor the future, nor any powers, neither height nor depth, nor anything else in all creation, will be able to separate us from the love of God that is in Christ Jesus our Lord. (Rom. 8:37-39)

Through the power of Christ, all are made powerful. Through the sacrifice of Jesus, the weak are transformed into conquerors! Jesus' underdog tale made all who are called to salvation "winners" and removed the scorn of sin and the shame of inadequacy. He replaced all of the negatives with under-the-surface possibility, and through His victory, Jesus made all underdogs capable. He replaced what they lacked in outside appearance with actual ability, true God-given capacity, to work and lead and perform in ways thought impossible by those detractors unable or unwilling to see God's handiwork in action. God's most amazing work is not reserved purely for those who appear to be most capable; His greatest work is reserved for all of those who are willing to submit, in all humility, and for those who would say, "I am not enough…use me, through *your power*, to accomplish great things *in your name*."

The Underdog Church-Planter

It's with these ideas in mind that this book is written. These words are meant for those called into ministry leadership, and specifically for those called to plant and replant churches, as a reminder that there is no disqualifier for you based upon your talents or seeming lack thereof. Instead, there is only hope and the inspiration to dream of what could be. This book is intended to be that encouraging voice whispering, "Maybe you can?"

As each author works to assist you in processing your *place* in ministry, your *drive* to see change, and your ability to *ignore* the skepticism of detractors, the goal is to see you humbly empowered to declare, "I am not enough but Jesus is!"

Over the past 15 years, as I have delved further and further into ministry leadership, I've witnessed the impossible too many times on both sides of the definition: I have watched as those deemed to have the most potential rise up and rally the masses...the talented, connected, and incredibly capable simply fail. Sadder still, too many times I have seen an amazing ascent turn into gut wrenching, disqualifying plummets towards dark and dismal places, dragging families and congregations through the mire of that failure. And shamefully, the entities that so often championed the incredible ascents were nowhere to be found in the accompanying plunge. I have also seen underdogs work below the surface of public notice, faithfully discharging their duties of love and care to unassuming people. I've seen individuals spoken about as those who carried so little talent, so little influence, and so little ability, it would be impossible for them to succeed. To some, a ministry of 25, 50, or 75 people could scarcely be considered "successful"; but these brave and faithful servants simply pursued their understood goals and submitted each day and each leadership opportunity *to the glory of God*.

In each of these impossible ideas, whether judged "triumphant success" or "miserable failure" the results remain the same: no matter the talent and in spite of the faults, God is the author of victory. You can be filled with all the talent in the world, but if you fail to modestly submit to the authority and majesty of Jesus, even if you win, *you lose*. On the contrary, you can bring nothing to the table, but if you carry the humble attitude of seeing yourself in light of God's grace, unworthy to be at the leadership table but willing to obey nonetheless...even if you don't succeed, as judged by the world around you, you are still a victorious champion.

So, here we go. Are you ready? We're about to embark on a journey that will ask you to dream bigger dreams, to attempt greater things, and to reinforce your character in ways in which some of you have never been challenged. For just a moment, we want to be the Mick to your *Rocky*...the Miyagi to your

Karate Kid… the Dumbledore to your *Harry Potter*. We want you to realize that you have worth. You may be an underdog…but God is not.

Right now, we're slow-clapping for you…

For Further Reflection

1. *Think of a time when you failed. How did it make you feel? What did you learn through that failure? About yourself? About God?*

2. *Have you ever thought about the "underdog" nature of Jesus or His Followers? Does this make him more attractive to you? Less?*

3. *When you think of the word "humility", what are three words that immediately come to mind? Is humility something you actively crave in your life? In those you work with?*

a theology for the underdog church-planter

Evan Skelton

"And I, when I came to you, brothers, did not come proclaiming to you the testimony of God with lofty speech or wisdom. For I decided to know nothing among you except Jesus Christ and him crucified. And I was with you in weakness and in fear and much trembling, and my speech and my message were not in plausible words of wisdom, but in demonstration of the Spirit and of power, so that your faith might not rest in the wisdom of men but in the power of God."

- The Apostle Paul (1 Cor. 2:1-5)

"I just don't know if I'm called to this."

David and I sat together, sipping coffee, as we do every week discussing family, friendship, and our pastoral work. An intern at a local church plant, David is occasionally entrusted to preach, and as he admitted, preaching can be a struggle for him. He doesn't consider himself a poor preacher. But, he finds the task to be sweaty work, and the finished product is rarely satisfying.

This particular Sunday felt worse than it had in a long while. Despite hours of prep, the sermon fell flat. It felt underwhelming and un-affecting at most. It is not that the sermon wasn't true. It is that it didn't seem... well... compelling.

To make matters worse, this church knows compelling preaching. Like David, the lead pastor is a careful exegete, but he is also charismatic. His sermons are winsome, sharp, and just plain funny. When he speaks, others are affected.

However, this experience is foreign to David. Instead, it felt as if he preached to empty seats. And, no matter how many hours he devoted, this

Sunday wasn't the exception to his preaching; it was the rule. The guilt of it seemed to squeeze his chest.

"I just don't know if I'm called to this."

Can you relate? It's not that your counsel isn't wise, but that it's quickly shrugged off. It's not that your outreach isn't strategic, but that no one seems to care. It is not that your discipleship is neglected, but that it is desperately slow. It's not that your sermons aren't true, but that they aren't compelling.

Perhaps, like David, your doubts concern a particular task like counseling, leadership, preaching or teaching, but perhaps your doubts go deeper. Perhaps, when it comes down to it, you are underwhelming.

Now, the elder's base level qualification is to be "above reproach," so if you are feeling "underwhelming," some serious evaluation is certainly warranted. We are never done repenting or receiving the correction of others, as sin will always be warring against our families, churches, and souls. Moreover, as those eager to deal well with what has been entrusted, we hold our practices and programs with open hands. If something isn't working, we need to seek Godly counsel. There is even a time to seriously question one's call to pastoral vocation. No one has the right to demand it, and whether due to unexpected circumstances, personal failure, or simply growing old, God will have you hand over the reigns or pull them from your grasp.

Yet, not every doubt is worth heeding. In fact, the sheer amount of biblical threads validating the underdog church-planter is staggering. It turns out that underwhelming, underdog church planting pastors are not only in great company; they are God's chosen means to show off. In this chapter, we will provide a brief (and certainly not comprehensive) overview of these foundations.

The God Who Makes Underdogs

I don't doubt that many reading this are skeptical that the Bible has much to say to the underdog church-planter. After all, isn't the Bible most concerned with the leaders who made an impact? Centuries later we know their names, heroes of the faith who,

...conquered kingdoms, enforced justice, obtained promises, stopped the mouths of lions, quenched the power of fire, escaped the edge of the sword, were made strong out of weakness, became mighty in war, put foreign armies to flight. (Hebrews 11:33b-34)

Even children know these heroes. Heroes like Elijah.

The Quiet Whisper

We know Elijah as the prophet who stood against the most vile monarchs in Israel's history, King Ahab and Queen Jezebel, and in so doing brings drought, resurrects the dead, even calls down fire from heaven.

But, on the other side of these events, we find a different Elijah, an Elijah in desperate circumstances on the other side of his greatest victory. In fact, the victory is only briefly enjoyed, as the bounty on his head is increased, setting him yet again on the run.

After days spent despairing of life, Elijah sets out. But, his eyes are not set toward Ahab; instead, they are focused south. Instead of running back to confront, he re-runs some old paths. They are the very paths Moses himself, the great prophet and deliverer of the law, arriving at his goal—the mountain the law itself was once delivered. Upon his arrival, God presses his servant, "What are you doing here, Elijah?" He answered:

I have been very jealous for the Lord, the God of hosts. For the people of Israel have forsaken your covenant, thrown down your altars, and killed your prophets with the sword, and I, even I only, am left, and they seek my life, to take it away. (1 Kings 19:10)

The accusation is striking, and by an external estimate, he seems to be right. Elijah is the faithful one among a horde of rebels, the new Moses watching Israel whore themselves to an idol. It is not difficult to imagine Elijah wondering whether it is time to start again, as God once offered Moses (Ex. 32:9-10), to make a great nation from his lonely, but faithful servant. Would God abandon his prophet, Israel's hope for salvation?

Instead of answering his accusation, God has Elijah stand on the mount that he might reveal himself as he did to Moses, but the difference between the two events is remarkable. As the text states, the LORD passed by, and a great and strong wind tore the mountains and broke in pieces the rocks before the LORD, but the LORD was not in the wind. And after the wind an earthquake, but the LORD was not in the earthquake. And after the earthquake a fire, but the LORD was not in the fire. And after the fire the sound of a low whisper. (1 Kings 19:11b-12)

God asks again, "What are you doing here, Elijah?" to which Elijah repeats his accusation, unaffected by the preceding scene. He sees himself alone, jealous for the LORD, woefully opposed and apparently forgotten.

God's response is unexpected. He doesn't grow angry with Elijah, but he also doesn't relent and promise renewed action on behalf of his people. Instead, he clarifies the point of the "gentle whisper."

He has not forgotten his people or his prophet, for that matter. In fact, he is working for their renewal, but through the very ordinary. First, it will be through ordinary means—through political process no less—not through spectacular demonstration, that God will work victory.[7]

Second and most importantly, Elijah has his facts wrong. God has "reserved" for himself many who have never bowed to Baal—7000, in fact—along with at least 100 prophets, kept alive though in hiding (1 Kings 18:13). Their names may be hidden and anonymous to Elijah, but they are crucial to God's plan.

Ian Provan says it well, speaking of God's strategy to save Israel:

From the beginning it had involved the gentle but devastating whisper as well as the all-consuming fire, the quiet ways of God's normal providence as well as the noisier ways of miraculous intervention. Elijah must be content with being *part* of the plan and not *the plan itself*.[8]

In fact, as if to drive this home, Elijah was then sent to anoint a successor.

A celebrity culture, such as ours, draws attention to big personalities, to massive ambitions, to "world-changing" strategies. But, more often than not, we belong to the normal, to the quiet whisper of God, to being part of the plan and not the plan itself. His plans are more "long term and more subtly conceived"[9] than we imagine, and our part is often temporary and hidden.

Underdogs and the Old Testament

God's preference for the weak and dependent, the "underdog," is a primary theme in the Old Testament. In fact, the theme is so dominant that is difficult to choose which examples to list. That being said, we will restrict our discussion to three categories—the underdog people, the underdog leaders, and the underdog message.

The Underdog People

Why did God choose Israel to be His people? Surely he should have run tryouts or something because Israel had neither military power nor industrial strength nor political influence. In fact, they were quite the opposite—a nation of despised slaves. Yet according to God, their weakness made them perfect for his plans:

> It was not because you were more in number than any other people that the Lord set his love on you and chose you, for you were the fewest of all peoples, but it is because the Lord loves you and is keeping the oath that he swore to your fathers, that the Lord has brought you out with a mighty hand and redeemed you from the house of slavery, from the hand of Pharaoh king of Egypt. (Deut. 7:7-8)

No skill, no beauty, no faith earned them God's attention. Rather, he "set" his love on them. Only a strong God would choose a weak people. Only a faithful God would choose a fickle people.

Moreover, he seems to keep this nation weak, placing them in circumstances way outside of their ability and requires his intervention. This is the people who were led from Egypt, the world powerhouse, their carts weighed down with its riches. This is the people who ran up against a sea only to walk through it! This is the people who crumbled a city just by circling its walls (Josh. 6:20). This is the people who conquered an army with hailstones and paused the sun to finish the fight (Josh. 10:11-14). This is the people who had the Assyrian horde perish *before* they crossed their doorstep (2 Kings 19:35). This is a people with great reason to say, "The king is not saved by his great army; a warrior is not delivered by his great strength… Behold, the eye of the Lord is on those who fear him, on those who hope in his steadfast love" (Ps. 33:16, 18).

Even when this nation turned its back on its strength, God was committed to their salvation crying, "I spread out my hands all the day to a rebellious people, who walk in a way that is not good, following their own devices" (Is. 65:2). Even when they are scattered in exile, God leads them home, determined to show off is his strength in their weakness.

The Underdog Leaders

God makes an equally strange choice in the leaders he chooses for his people. Even the "heroes of the faith" were unlikely and underwhelming in their own merit. Before Moses led the great Exodus and delivered the stone tablets, he was a fleeing man-killer "slow of speech and of tongue" (Ex. 4:10). Before David felled the giant or took the crown, he was least of his brothers, an unassuming shepherd, a wanted man on the run. Before Daniel evaded lions or looked into the future, he was stolen from his home and enslaved to the king's service. Before Ruth married Boaz and became a foremother of Jesus, she was a foreign widow wandering fields for her daily food.

His leaders weren't exactly moral giants either. Abraham gave away his wife. Judah slept with his daughter-in-law. Rahab was a prostitute. Gideon was a coward. Miriam spearheaded rebellion. Jephthah bargained away his daughter's life. Sampson was selfish & brutal. Balaam was a greed-hungry prophet-for-hire. David was a murdering adulterer.

Leave off their remarkable impact and these men and women are certainly unremarkable (or worse, remarkable for quite the wrong things). Yet as strange as God's choice of servants is, what he called them to is stranger.

The Underdog Message

God makes an underdog people, appoints underdog leaders, and then entrusts them with an underdog message—to repent and obey. It is a message on its own that is rarely received well, and then it receives some very strange packaging.

First, think of the **methods**. There is the simple strangeness of preaching, often to small and sneering crowds. Then, there is the symbolic declaration of Sabbath, dietary restrictions, and circumcision! Sometimes, the means are even more… well… weird… like Elijah who playacted God's judgement. He was made unable to speak, left lying on his side for over a year, made to shave his head and burn the hair, even disallowed from mourning his dead wife. Or there is Hosea, who demonstrated the strength of God's love and the pain of Israel's betrayal by marrying a prostitute. If God wanted his message to be received, surely there are better means. Maybe a Netflix movie.

Often, the **timing** is strange as well. There is Joseph who lived a life of obscurity, wrongfully jailed and forgotten, before gaining any real influence. And there is Samuel who started influential, even anointing Israel's first kings, but faded into insignificance decades before his death. Then consider Jeremiah who began his ministry knowing they were only years from exile.

Equally strange is the **context** in which his leaders ministered. There is Jonah who would not lead Israel's renewal but was called instead to their fiercest enemies, known for their violent power. There is Nehemiah, who lived in prestige as cupbearer to the king but was called instead to go home and rebuild ruined walls. And, there is Elijah, who actually spent very little of his ministry in proclamation but was mostly on the run or hiding under a foreign widow's roof.

Now we might say any strange methods, timing, or context are worth it, so long as the **fruit** is significant. But, the fruit makes even less sense. In fact, their most common fruit was to be overlooked and opposed. Isaiah in his very call was instructed, "Make the heart of this people dull, and their ears heavy, and blind their eyes" (Is. 6:10a). In Jeremiah's call he was told curtly, "They will fight against you" (Jer. 1:19). In fact, the one thing that seems to unite every prophet is the opposition they faced. Sometimes it was the opposition of abuse or death, but more often they were simply ignored (see Matt. 5:12; Acts 7:52).

Confirming that Scriptures are hardly preoccupied with celebrity comes Hebrews 11, the heroes of faith text I referenced before, which makes a sudden turn:

> ...Some were tortured, refusing to accept release, so that they might rise again to a better life. Others suffered mocking and flogging, and even chains and imprisonment. They were stoned, they were sawn in two, they were killed with the sword. They went about in skins of sheep and goats, destitute, afflicted, mistreated—of whom the world was not worthy—wandering about in deserts and mountains, and in dens and caves of the earth. (Heb. 11:35b-38)

Do you notice these faithful are nameless? God so often preserves his Word by means of the anonymous... by those who live and die obscure to the world but known to him. In fact, it seems God imposes limits upon his servants. He restricts their capacity and restrains their influence, so that the nations would hope in no one else.

The Underdogs Who Want More

The thing about underdogs, though, is we don't expect them to stay underdogs. Rocky takes the great Apollo. The Jamaicans win bobsledding gold. A "slumdog" becomes a millionaire. We love stories where the underdog becomes the top dog. But, an underdog that stays an underdog? Talk about a box office flop.

We might admit to be underdogs, but the truth is, we don't want to say there. We fight. We don't like to be underwhelming. Instead of leaning into our (apparent) weakness as a people, we idolize strength, power, and success. We lose the biblical distinctiveness we fear is losing us ground and overemphasize the business strategies we are sure will gain it back.

Instead of resting in our (apparent) weakness as leaders, we become zealous for image, building ministry upon personalities and envying those who steal attention away. We are hesitant to hand leadership (and certainly not the pulpit) over to others, particularly those of higher capacity.

Instead of embracing the (apparent) weakness of our message, we avoid difficult demands and doctrines, save those that are sure to get "amens" from the pews. Instead, we replace true health with legalism or clever programming, both of which can be deceptively successful.

Notice, the weakness is only "apparent." For, it is in weakness and dependence that God best shows off his strength. So why do we, the underdogs, want more?

Maybe the factors are external… People have moved on from your ministry to the next cool thing. You have been unjustly criticized for your "lack of fruit" or even let go for the sake of ministry "growth." Or, maybe the factors are internal… Your threatened pride has made you fearful and envious or even defeated and bitter.

Underdogs longing to be top dogs not only miss the beauty of their role, they miss opportunities to show off true strength. In this case, I have much more in common with God's enemies, as well as their fate. Like Saul, we cling to our crown but will fall on our spear. Like Nebuchadnezzar, we boast in our glory but will be left munching grass. Like Herod, we welcome worship but will be eaten alive.

This is why the pastoral code makes sure to disallow arrogance (see 1 Pet. 5:15; Titus 1:7). Whether you self-despise or self-promote, pride is our fight. *Who will vindicate the despised? Who will humble the arrogant?*

The God Who Became an Underdog

> For he grew up before him like a young plant, and like a root out of dry ground; he had no form or majesty that we should look at him, and no beauty that we should desire him. He was despised and rejected by men; a man of sorrows, and acquainted with grief; and as one from whom men hide their faces. He was despised, and we esteemed him not. Surely he has borne our griefs and carried our sorrows; yet we esteemed him stricken, smitten by God, and afflicted. (Is. 53:2-4)

To know weakness and dependence is to see Jesus, the only One who ever embraced it. When God became man, he was born from a weak line (just think of the women Matthew mentions—Tamar, Rahab, Ruth, Bathsheba, and Mary) (Matt. 1:3, 5, 6, 16) to a weak people (again occupied by the world power of the time) in weak circumstances (to poor parents in a feeding trough only to be celebrated social outcasts). And, what job does God hand him? He works as a common carpenter… for 30 years.

When his public ministry does come about, he identifies more with the suffering servant than the conquering king. In fact, he advocates weakness, saying things like, "Truly, I say to you, unless you turn and become like children, you will never enter the kingdom of heaven," and, "If anyone would come after me, let him deny himself and take up his cross and follow me. For whoever would save his life will lose it, but whoever loses his life for my sake will find it" (Matt. 18:3b; 16:24-25). In fact, he goes as far as to say, ""Woe to you, when all people speak well of you, for so their fathers did to the false prophets" (Luke 6:26).

More than that, he spends time with the weak. The blind, the lame, the mourning, the poor, the outcast, the sick, the tax collectors and sinners—these are his company. And his message, like the prophets of old, was rejected more than it was received. In fact, one of the reasons he speaks in parables was that, "they may indeed see but not perceive, and may indeed hear but not understand, lest they should turn and be forgiven" (Mark 4:12 ; cf. Is. 6:9). At one point so many turned in offense of his claims that he looks to the Twelve and asks, "Do you want to go away as well?" (John 6:67b).

Ultimately, he would die in weakness, as if forgotten by all. He faced baseless accusations and ruthless mocking. He was abandoned by those who followed him, denied by those who knew him, scorned by those who didn't. And worst of all, on the cross, the Father forsook his Son. The true King was treated like a pretender to the throne.

Why? It was not simply to identify with our weakness, but to pay the penalty of our pride. Every jealous comment, every fearful decision, every self-promoting strategy, every discontented distraction—Jesus bore the punishment it was due. He came to the end of the road our idols have paved. D.A. Carson summarizes this well:

> Jesus cries this cry, "My God! I am forsaken!" so that for all eternity Don Carson will not have to. Hear the ironies of the cross:
>
> 1. The man who is mocked as king—is king.
> 2. The man who is utterly powerless—is powerful.
> 3. The man who can't save himself—saves others.
> 4. The man who cries out in despair—trusts God.[10]

In his abject weakness, Jesus both showed and *accomplished* God's strength. For, praise God, the story doesn't end with his humiliation. What then would be the hope for our sin and our suffering? Instead, just when it seemed his very memory would perish, he flipped a "might-makes-right" world on its head. The mocked King takes up his rule. In fact, he takes beggars, such as I, to share his spoils of war. I, enemy of the state, am given dignity and significance, promised to blossom for all eternity. By faith in his perfect strength (rather than feeble competitors), all pride is deflated and significance comes to the insignificant. Even the most marginal finds belonging, and the ugliest weakness finds purpose.

The God Who Restores Underdogs

Immediately, we see the impacts of this new life Christ brings. The same disciples who vied for power take instead the cup of weakness (see Matt. 20:20-28 and Mark 10:35-45). The same disciples who fear opposition, sing hymns in prison (see Acts 16:25). The same disciples who run from Jesus' death run towards their own. Even when writing the New Testament, they don't paint over their failures and are instead content to make much of Jesus.

One of the clearest pictures of this comes from the life of Paul. Talk about a strange choice for a messenger. Paul admits, "...I am the least of the apostles, unworthy to be called an apostle, because I persecuted the church of God" (1 Cor. 15:9). And, lest someone assert his present significance, he adds, "But by the grace of God I am what I am..." (1 Cor. 15:10a).

Concerning God's methods, Paul says much of his ministry was, "in weakness and in fear and much trembling" (1 Cor. 2:3). And God's timing, Paul was sent away (along with Barnabas) just as "the word of God increased and multiplied," right when good leadership was most needed (Acts 12:25). Moreover, a main context of his ministry was in prison with only Roman soldiers as an audience. But, at least the fruit was always great, right?

> Five times I received at the hands of the Jews the forty lashes less one. Three times I was beaten with rods. Once I was stoned. Three times I was shipwrecked; a night and a day I was adrift at sea; on frequent journeys, in danger from rivers, danger from robbers, danger from my own people, danger from Gentiles, danger in the city, danger in the wilderness, danger at sea, danger from false brothers; in toil and hardship, through many a sleepless night, in hunger and thirst, often without food, in cold and exposure. And, apart from other things, there is the daily pressure on me of my anxiety for all the churches. (2 Cor. 11:24-28)

Even the great sermon of Mars Hill resulted in only "some men" who joined him and believed (Acts 17:34).

As Paul says, "Who is weak, and I am not weak?" (2 Cor. 11:29a). In fact, here was a man who when others would call him unimpressive, even weak and foolish, would not defend himself. Rather, not only did their doubt not surprise him; he celebrated it:

> And I, when I came to you, brothers, did not come proclaiming to you the testimony of God with lofty speech or wisdom. For I decided to know nothing among you except Jesus Christ and him crucified. And I was with you in weakness and in fear and much trembling, and my speech and my message were not in plausible words of wisdom, but in demonstration of the Spirit and of power, so that your faith might not rest in the wisdom of men but in the power of God. (1 Cor. 2:1-5)

He recognizes that we all are only servants carrying out our assigned tasks, God's fellow workers, stewards of mysteries of God (1 Cor. 3:5-9). Koessler calls this "The No-Little-Places Principle: Wherever God has called me to minister is an important place."[11] Or, as Dr. Warren Wiersbe has often said, "In the eyes of God there are no small churches, nor are there big preachers."[12]

Importantly, whatever ministry Paul did have was deeply dependent upon nameless elder/pastors. While he planted the seed, there were others who watered. Though he laid the foundation, there are untold others who built upon it (see Acts 14:23; cf. 1 Cor. 3:5-8).

It was nameless elders that preserved the doctrine of the church at the Jerusalem Council (Acts 15). And when Paul departed for his eventual arrest in Jerusalem, it was into the hands of nameless elders he entrusted the church (Acts 20:17-38).

We have inherited their role. "Clothed in humility" we…

> …shepherd the flock of God that is among you, exercising oversight, not under compulsion, but willingly, as God would have you; not for shameful gain, but eagerly; not domineering over those in your charge, but being examples to the flock. And when the chief Shepherd appears, you will receive the unfading crown of glory. (1 Pet. 5:2-4)

Notice that this passage prevents our underdog identity from becoming an excuse, particularly for laziness, indifference, or spitefulness. Nor does it excuse us from creativity, thoughtfulness, and zeal. Let's make sure it is actually the offense of the cross that others stumble over, and let's give balanced attention to strategic discipleship, persuasive evangelism, even websites and branding. But, that being said, would you with Paul, feely admit, "We have become, and are still, like the scum of the world, the refuse of all things"(1 Cor. 4:13)? Will you, too, draw limits around your ministry knowing that, as Carson points out, "As long as people are impressed by your powerful personality and impressive gifts, there is very little room for you to impress them with a crucified Savior."[13] Would you "boast all the more gladly of my weaknesses, so that the power of Christ may rest upon me," knowing that, "*when* I am weak, *then* I am strong" (2 Cor. 12:9b, 10b)?

Conclusion

In closing, one of the clearest demonstrations of this to me comes from the book, *Memoirs of an Ordinary Pastor*.

Tom Carson was, as his son puts, an ordinary pastor. He was not extraordinarily gifted, never rose far in his denomination, never wrote a book, never was a far-sighted visionary nor a gifted administrator. Tom was an ordinary pastor who labored long in his work.

Tom served in Montreal at a time when Protestants were rare and opposed, while his own work was slow and plodding. *For 60 years*, he served small and unimpressive churches, where numbers hovered on the lower end of double digits. He struggled with intense private frustration and deep depression. At one point, he was met with very cruel, very public, very unwarranted accusation. His pastoral work came to an abrupt end as his wife began the 8-year descent of Alzheimer's disease. He would die 3 years later, alone in his hospital bed.

If Tom Carson was at all unique, it was in his anonymous faithfulness. He labored long in unremarkable ministry, but to those closest to him, including the son who wrote his biography, he was known as a man who was early and often in prayer, quick to laugh and slow to criticize, a lover of the Bible, a servant of people, a caring father, an attentive husband, a humble man devoted to the fame of Jesus.

Don closes the biography of his dad with the following words:

> When he died, there were no crowds outside the hospital, no editorial comments in the papers, no announcements on the television, no mention in Parliament, no attention paid by the nation. In his hospital room there was no one by his bedside. There was only the quiet hiss of oxygen, vainly venting because he had stopped breathing and would never need it again.

> But on the other side, all the trumpets sounded. Dad won entrance to the only throne-room that matters, not because he was a good man or a great man—he was, after all, a most ordinary pastor—but because he was a forgiven man. And he heard the voice of him whom he longed to hear saying, "Well done, good and faithful servant; enter into the joy of your Lord."[14]

For Further Reflection

Read 1 Corinthians 1-4.

1. *In what ways does our celebrity culture encourage a similar division to that described in these chapters, particularly in the church?*

2. *What pressures, desires, and lies tempt you to throw off your identity as an underdog church-planter?*

3. *If the apostle Paul took an honest look at your ministry, what would he say your confidence was in? What would he say your ministry is built upon?*

4. *How would your life look different if you believed Wiersbe's quote, "In the eyes of God there are no small churches, nor are there big preachers"?*

a look at the first underdog church-planters

Matt Whitt

"But God chose the foolish things of the world to shame the wise; God chose the weak things of the world to shame the strong."

- The Apostle Paul (1 Cor. 1:27)

When we talk about Underdog Church-Planters, we are getting at the heart of what God is looking for in those He calls to plant a church. What He is looking for and ultimately what He is preparing and working in our hearts. We are speaking about God-called and Spirit-gifted leaders. So first, let us be careful implying that none of us are qualified to lead a church; if that were the case, we would not be doing so. False humility has no place in church planting just as pride has no place in church planting. And so, being clear, while apart from Christ none of us have any business leading a church plant or replant, we who have been called are qualified because Christ is qualified and makes us so when we abide in Him. Any quality or giftedness we have is not our own but has been placed there by God. This is true for the first church-planters as well. Those first apostles who ventured out to hostile cities and distant lands… Those people who began a church that, if based on their own efforts and abilities, never would have made it.

It would be easy to address this topic by taking examples from these men's lives from before they were Christians and discuss how unqualified they were to do the Lord's work. It would be easy, but probably unhelpful. And so, first, what this chapter is not:

#1. This chapter is not a look at the pre-resurrection mistakes, personalities, and sins that would have otherwise disqualified the disciples and Paul from leadership. For example, Peter's hot-headedness that caused even Jesus to publicly scold him, Thomas' doubt that Jesus had actually been raised from the dead, and Saul's (pre-Paul) personal crusade to stamp out the movement of Christ before it could take root. I am sure that if you looked into the background of any— even the best — of those God called to lead His church, we would see the same thing: sin, because we are all sinners. But when an individual repents of past sins and receives salvation they become a Christian, not an underdog church-planter. There have been many church-planters with sinful pasts, who were redeemed by Christ who did not become underdog church-planters.

#2. This chapter is not a sometimes-cliché and token reminder that every person God used to build and grow His church had continuing flaws. For example, Paul's apparently boring and long sermons that put a young man to sleep causing him to fall out a window and die (Acts 20:7-12). Or the wonderful occasion when Paul and Barnabas were mistaken for Zeus and Hermes (Acts 14). We like to remember these things because we identify with them. It somehow makes our own foibles and faults, mistakes and blunders seem somehow, maybe, not so bad. But, it does not take an underdog church-planter to do these kinds of things, everyone does.

We know these men made mistakes, we know they were not perfect. If it was not their imperfection that made them Underdog Church-Planters, then what was it? Here are five underdog characteristics of the early church-planters. These five are not exhaustive in making an underdog church-planter, as evidenced by rest of the chapters in this book. However, they are what I think is clearly seen in the lives and the stories of the first church-planters and may help us think through our own lives to see if we have been called similarly to be underdog church-planters.

Before we begin, let me say that we are not going to be looking much at the Apostle Paul. For some this may be a glaring omission. Do we think Paul was not an underdog church-planter? No, he probably was. Despite his prominence to us, and even at that time in history, it is clear from his life and teaching that he fit the characteristics of an underdog church-planter. Let this be a reminder that underdog does not mean unsuccessful (by human standards), or unknown.

Underdog Planters Let Others Finish the Work They Started

> Philip went down to the city of Samaria and proclaimed to them the Christ. And the crowds with one accord paid attention to what was being said by Philip when they heard him and saw the signs that he did. For unclean spirits, crying out with a loud voice, came out of many who had them, and many who were paralyzed or lame were healed. So there was much joy in that city. (Acts 8:5-8)

This is such a great testimony to what Philip the deacon, later called Philip the Evangelist, was able to do in ministry. We see his willingness to go someplace others had likely not wanted to go. We see his ability to draw the full attention of crowds and then do some pretty amazing things. However, he is not able to do everything. The people believe, they are baptized in the name of Jesus, they are saved, but a few verses later we see that they need to be brought into the unity of the church.

> Now when the apostles at Jerusalem heard that Samaria had received the word of God, they sent to them Peter and John, who came down and prayed for them that they might receive the Holy Spirit, for he had not yet fallen on any of them, but they had only been baptized in the name of the Lord Jesus. Then they laid their hands on them and they received the Holy Spirit. (Acts 8:14-17)

Have you ever wondered why Philip, despite being full of the Holy Spirit, gifted as a communicator, and gifted to perform some very miraculous signs is unable to effectively finish the Gospel work? The Holy Spirit is delayed in coming on them until Peter and John arrive. This is a necessary step to make sure the Samaritans, who had previously been excluded from salvation in the Jewish faith, could be accepted as part of the one family of God in Christ. This was "no small step towards a people who were regarded as apostate 'untouchables.'"[15] Philip brings the Samaritans into the faith, but it is only when Peter and John come with the full authority from Jerusalem that the Samaritans are brought into the church. This is a distinction we do not need today, but was important for the unity of the infant Christian church.

Philip knew his role and must have known how important Peter and John were in completing the work he had begun. Underdog church-planters know that the glory belongs to God and he will use whomever he wants in whatever way he desires. At times that may mean we begin a work that others will finish later.

I am reminded of the story of Nate Saint and Jim Elliott, missionaries to the Auca Indians in Ecuador. Five missionary men passionate about God, desiring to show the love of God to a violent people, were slaughtered by those people. But just a few years later some of their wives were able to reach those same people with the Gospel and bring the entire tribe into saving faith of Jesus Christ. Their wives finished a work that they had begun and were able to plant a church that never should have been by earthly standards. Are we willing to let others finish the work we begin? Are we willing to let others take the credit for things we started, labored in, but were unable to finish?

Underdog Church-Planters Are Okay with Obscurity

Do you realize that most of the disciples never get mentioned in Scripture after Acts 1:13, even though according to history, all of them continued to serve the Lord, minister in his name, and evangelize until martyrdom or a natural death took them? This is because they were willing to go to whatever place God called them, even if it meant their names and deeds would not be widely noticed or found in scripture again. Andrew, Philip (not the Evangelist), Thomas, Bartholomew, Matthew, James the son of Alpheaus, Simon the Zealot, and Judas the son of James are never mentioned again in the Bible. Even Peter, James, and John do not get much more ink time. We read of James' martyrdom in Acts 12:2 and then he is not mentioned again. With the exception of his two letters, Peter's name fades out by the end of Acts. Even John's name is never seen again, apart from his Gospel, letters, and the book of Revelation. We simply do not know what they did or accomplished after these early chapters in Acts.

Underdog church-planters must be willing to let others' names become great while their names may remain unknown. There is a quote often attributed to C.S. Lewis but whose author is unknown: "Don't think less about yourself, but think about yourself less." We need to be willing to enter obscurity for the sake of being faithful.

I am writing these words from the town of La Junta, Colorado. This year I was called to this town I had never heard of, to replant a church that has never made much of a mark outside of the small town where it has been a fixture for over a century. We are not, and likely never will be, known as even a shadow in comparison to Bethlehem Baptist Church (John Piper), Redeemer Presbyterian (Timothy Keller), or The Village Church (Matt Chandler). But my prayer is that we will be well known as Gospel-preaching lovers of Jesus in our small town and the valley that surrounds us. By the way, the permission to stop striving to be one of "the greats", and to simply be a regular faithful pastor in a regular faithful church was the most freeing gift I received since the day I was given salvation by the Lord.

Joseph Tenney wrote, "If you're a pastor, perhaps make a fresh effort to stop pursuing your own renown. Stop building your platform. Will God raise up voices and songs and messages for his purposes that are greater than our originally intended purposes? Absolutely. But when he does, we should be able to tell that God did it, not us. Let him make you known outside of himself and his church if he so desires."[16] The underdog church-planter lets God make of him what God wants to make of him. For some that means being well-known, but for most of us this means obscurity.

Underdog Planters Are Ready to be Used By God

When I read the book of Acts, I see people who are in the right place at the right time. Is this good human planning, or the work of the Holy Spirit? The answer is, of course, both. The Apostles are where they are supposed to be, and that is where they encounter ministry opportunities. In some cases they are led there by specific guidance of the Holy Spirit, such as we see with Philip in Acts 8:26-27a, "Now an angel of the Lord said to Philip, "Rise and go toward the south to the road that goes down from Jerusalem to Gaza." This is a desert place. And he rose and went." At other times, we simply see the Apostles encountering a person in need. In Acts 3:1-6 Peter and John meet a crippled man and heal him. When they do so they are, "going up to the temple at the hour of prayer." We see something similar in Acts 16 when Paul and Barnabas encounter a demon-possessed slave girl and provide deliverance. In both cases, the Apostles are where they are supposed to be, and because of that, the Lord uses them to effect miracles for people in desperate need. They did not know how God was going to use them on this particular day, but they were ready for whatever He intended. They were in place and willing to engage with those they encountered as they went.

The full weight of the great commission is that we are to be making disciples, "as we go." We cannot do this from our home offices or even our church offices. It is easy for most of us to go about our day either too busy or too focused to notice the people around us, if we even have the chance to encounter someone who might be in need of hearing or being shown the Gospel. Our culture does not make it easy to meet people on any given day. "Going" for us may mean we need to walk to our places of work, or to the bus stop to ride along with other people. We may need eat lunch in a diner or in a nearby park and when we go home, take our kids out to a park instead of watching television. Underdog church-planters know they need to be out and about, listening to the Holy Spirit about where to go next.

Underdog Church-Planters Keep Teaching and Building Up

> Some time later Paul said to Barnabas, "Let us go back and visit the brothers in all the towns where we preached the word of the Lord and see how they are doing." Barnabas wanted to take John, also called Mark, with them, but Paul did not think it wise to take him, because he had deserted them in Pamphylia and had not continued with them in the work. They had such a sharp disagreement that they parted company. Barnabas took Mark and sailed for Cyprus. (Acts 15:36-39a)

In this single act, Barnabas chooses the hard road of leaving a friend. The book of Acts follows Paul's ministry forward and Barnabas is not in it anymore. For any of us that have had a parting of ways with a partner in ministry or a mentor, we may find ourselves saddened by this split, as we probably should be. But something else is going on here. We can be sure that Barnabas would have liked to stay with Paul, to continue serving with his friend, but he saw another need… the need to give his cousin Mark another chance. This act cost him dearly, but built-up Mark. Though we only read of one positive but fairly ambiguous reference to Barnabas by Paul in his later writings (1 Cor 9:6), Paul references Mark three times in his letters, all in a positive light, and Peter refers to Mark as a son (1 Peter 5:13). It is reasonable to assume that without Barnabas's encouragement and mentoring, we never would have heard Mark's name another time in scripture either. Barnabas lays down his own interests and even his relationship with Paul for the sake of teaching and encouraging Mark.

The underdog church-planter knows there is not a lot of glory in building others up, but does it for their good and for God's glory. We should be quick to pour into those individuals in who we see potential.

Underdog Church-Planters are Teachable

> Now a Jew named Apollos, a native of Alexandria, came to Ephesus. He was an eloquent man, competent in the Scriptures. He had been instructed in the way of the Lord. And being fervent in spirit, he spoke and taught accurately the things concerning Jesus, though he knew only the baptism of John. He began to speak boldly in the synagogue, but when Priscilla and Aquila heard him, they took him aside and explained to him the way of God more accurately. And when he wished to cross to Achaia, the brothers encouraged him and wrote to the disciples to welcome him. When he arrived, he greatly helped those who through grace had believed, for he powerfully refuted the Jews in public, showing by the Scriptures that the Christ was Jesus. (Acts 18:24-28)

I think this story of Apollos is one of my favorite snippets from the book of Acts. We might ask so many questions of this passage, but all of them get lost in the simple fact that Apollos allows Priscilla and Aquila to mentor and teach him, and his ministry effectiveness increases as a direct result. His fervent spirit (verse 25) and boldness (verse 26) are changed into power (verse 28) through more accurate teaching.

When I was in high school I joined the track team. I was not a great sprinter nor was I a good distance runner. The reality is that I was not a great runner at all, but I tried really hard. At one point, I ended up on a relay team for the 200. I think I was the number two runner. As our first runner approached me, ready to hand off the baton, I began moving forward, exactly as I was supposed to do. However, my excitement got the best of me and I began moving too quickly. Our first runner, at the end of his energy, having pushed with every bit of energy to get to me, was unable to close the gap between us and in a desperate attempt to pass the baton he lunged forward. He threw himself towards me, but it was futile. I was too far away. He crashed and burned, the baton went skidding across the ground, and I had to recover it in order to keep running. He was hurt, and we lost the the race.

Many of us start out this way in ministry. Passion, excitement, and energy oozing from our every action. We run out the door thinking we are going to take on the devil and win souls for Jesus. But as soon as the excitement wears off, a mountain of a problem shows up, or some challenge arises, we realize we started too quickly and lack something we need in order to do well. Either we hurt someone or are hurt ourselves in the process.

My guess is that we have all heard that ministry is a marathon, not a sprint. Most of us could sprint 100 yards if we needed to. Maybe not fast… we wouldn't win a race against a trained runner, but we could complete it. However, if asked to run a marathon without training, sustenance, and encouragement very few of would be able to cross the finish line, some of us would kill ourselves trying.

This is why I love the story of Apollos, because I see hope not only for myself but also for so many whose passion, excitement, and calling get the best of them. But because they are teachable, they are able to recover and their effectiveness is increased.

Like Apollos, when correction, training, or teaching comes, *listen*. No one likes to be criticized; no one likes to be shown weak areas in their lives or in their ministry. But, when it comes, receive it. And do not just passively wait for it; seek it out, surround yourself with people who will help you grow, who will encourage you and challenge you.

Of each of these five characteristics we see in the underdog church-planters from the early church, teachability is likely the most important because without it most of what you will read in this book won't matter. I hope the reason you're reading any of this is because, in some way, you desire to learn and be taught.

For Further Reflection

1. *Which of these stories and traits do you most identify with?*

2. *Which of these traits is a challenge for you? How can you pursue being like these first underdog church-planters?*

3. *What other underdog traits do you see in the first church-planters we read about it in the book of Acts?*

priorities
of the underdog church-planter

the underdog church-planter as...
dependent disciple

Jeff Jung

"As many have learned and later taught, you don't realize Jesus is all you need until Jesus is all you have."

- Timothy Keller

Do you remember your first job? When I was sixteen, I got a job at a local grocery store. I remember my first day of training. I was a cashier. After an hour of training, I was left alone to manage everything. I knew how to use a cash register to make a sale, take their money, give them their change and a receipt, wrap or bag their purchase, handle returns and exchanges, but I had no idea how to use the intercom for announcements. To be more accurate, I knew how to use it, but I was just too nervous to do it. I was terrified by the fact that everyone could hear me talking. I remember a customer needed something and I had to page someone over the intercom. The thought of using it made me so nervous that I picked up the phone and froze. Awkward silence for a while until the customer said, "Are you okay? You can put down the phone." I was in way over my head.

We can all remember the first time we were put in a position of responsibility, knowing that we could blow it. It may have been a job or maybe looking after children. It was likely a time when we were left alone and in charge, and we weren't sure we were ready.

This chapter is all about the Underdog Church-Planter as Dependent Disciple. What does it look like for a church-planter to solely rely on the power and the wisdom of God as a God-reliant disciple not a self-reliant disciple? For this subject matter, I'd like for us to consider a passage in the Gospel of Mark, where the disciples were in over their heads for the job they have given by

Jesus. I think this is one of the key episodes in the training of the disciples, and also a key story in teaching us, underdog church-planters, something that we really need to understand from God's perspective on the job we have been entrusted with by Him.

In Mark 3:13-15 and 6:7, Jesus had given His chosen disciples authority to cast out demons:

> Jesus went up on a mountainside and called to him those he wanted, and they came to him. He appointed twelve that they might be with him and that he might send them out to preach and to have authority to drive out demons. (Mark 3:13-15)

> Calling the Twelve to him, he began to send them out two by two and gave them authority over evil spirits. (Mark 6:7)

The disciples were left alone to do ministry both preaching the gospel of the kingdom of God and, with a given authority from Jesus over evil spirits, to deal with demons while He was gone. In Mark 9:14-29, Jesus comes back and found out that the disciples failed to cast out the demon from a son the father brought before them. It was chaos. You think it's a bad idea to leave me in charge of cash register all by myself, imagine being left by Jesus to minister in His absence. If that's not enough, imagine dealing with demons and evil spirits. Jesus was definitely preparing them, but they weren't ready yet.

We need to look at this passage because we are in a very similar situation. Church planting is hard, very hard. Though underdog church-planters trust God has called them into ministry, it is a lonely job. It's for this reason the ministry shouldn't be viewed as a career, but a calling that's dependent on God. The enemy will attack us – he doesn't want God's kingdom to expand! But Jesus does and promises to be with us. Jesus promised us in the Great Commission that He will be with us always to the end of the age because He knows that we can't do anything apart from His presence in our lives (Matthew 28:18-20). God is calling us to draw near to Him and depend on Him for all things.

This passage from Mark 9:14-29 teaches us three lessons that we need to know as a dependent disciple and as an underdog church-planter. First, we're faced with situations in ministry that are greater than we can handle. Second, we have a tendency to be self-reliant instead of God-reliant. Finally, God calls us to repent and depend on Him for everything.

So let's look at these together, beginning with the first lesson we need to learn.

1. We're faced with situations in ministry that are greater than we can handle.

We're continually faced with situations in ministry that are greater than we can handle. Mark describes the scene in 9:14-18:

> "When they came to the other disciples, they saw a large crowd around them and the teachers of the law arguing with them. As soon as all the people saw Jesus, they were overwhelmed with wonder and ran to greet him." What are you arguing with them about?" he asked. A man in the crowd answered, "Teacher, I brought you my son, who is possessed by a spirit that has robbed him of speech. Whenever it seizes him, it throws him to the ground. He foams at the mouth, gnashes his teeth and becomes rigid. I asked your disciples to drive out the spirit, but they could not."

What is the situation that the disciples faced? The disciples were put in a situation to act as representatives of Jesus, to carry out His ministry. This is exactly the situation that you and I are in as well.

But what did the disciples soon discover? They discovered the limitations of their ability to act as representatives of Jesus. They were faced with a boy possessed with an evil spirit. We read in verses 21 and 22 that this spirit had been tormenting the boy since childhood. In Mark 9:22, we are told that the demon "has often thrown him into fire or water to kill him." Scripture is clear that evil does exist, and Satan is intent on destroying and killing, and this boy had been dealing with this his entire life. So, the disciples were facing a spiritual battle, human need, and extraordinary difficulty that was beyond their own resources. This is, by the way, is the exact same thing we face every day as we carry out His ministry. Indeed, the struggle is greater in the arena of church planting.

I've been thinking lately about some of the struggles and challenges I've encountered as a church-planter. I have been commissioned to act as His representative, and He has given me authority. But when I look around, I'm overwhelmed by the needs around me, feeling inadequate, sometimes helpless, to take on the responsibility and serve well. These disciples encountered the boy tormented with an evil spirit. I've also encountered all kinds of issues that are far beyond what I can handle: people who are in spiritual bondage, those suffering with sicknesses, and marriages that are in trouble. I look around and see people living in impossible situations, such as people caught in addiction, or living in violent and abusive situations.

Now here's what I often do when I'm in that place feeling overwhelmed and inadequate by the needs around me. I take a moment and pause, and see the enormity of what has been set before me. Then I remind myself of this truth, "What Jesus has called me to do is humanly impossible." I can't preach a sermon that can change your life. I can't deal with a situation like the disciples were dealing with on my own. He has called me to tasks beyond my abilities. No doubt, we're faced with situations in ministry that are greater than we can handle. So, where do we turn when we come to this realization?

2. We have a tendency to be self-reliant instead of God-reliant.

We need to see that this passage teaches us that we have a tendency to be self-reliant instead of God-reliant. You'd think we would know that we need to depend on God to get anything done, but we have this tendency to rely on our own strength. We spend a lot of time persuading others that we're knowledgeable and competent; proving ourselves that we have what it takes for this job of ministry. We have a really hard time admitting that we are dependent on God rather than our own strength and techniques.

Picture the scene as Jesus comes to where the crowd was gathered. The disciples have failed publicly. There's nothing like being surrounded by a crowd while you fall flat on your face. The scribes are arguing with the disciples. The father is frustrated, and the boy is no better. It's…chaos.

What did Jesus say? He says in Mark 9:19, "You unbelieving generation…how long shall I stay with you? How long shall I put up with you?" Do you get the impression that Jesus is frustrated? It's interesting that He talks about an unbelieving *generation*, which implies that Jesus didn't only have a problem with the disciples, the problem is with everyone in that generation. In other words, this isn't a problem that's restricted to a few people. This is a problem that really affects everyone, which includes us as well.

What's the problem? Was the demon too powerful? There's no doubt that this demon was powerful. Later Jesus says, "This kind can come out only by prayer" (Mark 9:29) implying that this is a difficult case. The disciples had been able to cast out other demons before, but this was a more difficult demon.

But the problem, according to Jesus, wasn't really the demon. Jesus doesn't get frustrated with the demon. In fact, He had no problem with the demon. The problem is that the disciples' *faith* is too small. The problem isn't the demon; the problem is the disciples. The problem isn't the difficult situations we face in ministry; it's us. The disciples were trying to handle things on their own. We try to take matters into our own hands. This passage shows us two ways, a right way and a wrong way, to handle the situation. So let me explain.

First, let's see the wrong way we handle ministry. Where did the disciples fail? Listen to verses 28 and 29. "After Jesus had gone indoors, his disciples asked him privately, "Why couldn't we drive it out?" He replied, "This kind can come out only by prayer." This is shocking. It looks like the disciples relied on their own devices to handle the demon. How do we know that? We know it because they didn't rely on God's strength and power *through prayer* but rather the focus was on themselves, and therefore, they asked Jesus, "why couldn't *we* drive it out?" But let's think about that a bit more. How many times have we tried to serve others with the same self-reliance as the disciples did? Could it be that this is one of the reasons for our lack of power? Could this be a reason we don't see God's extraordinary work in the power of the Holy Spirit in our churches?

Os Guinness believes,

> The two most easily recognizable hallmarks of secularization are the exaltation of numbers and technique. Both are prominent in the church-growth movement. In its fascination with statistics and data at the expense of truth, this movement is characteristically modern...In a world of number crunchers, bean counters, and computer analysts, the growth of churches as a measurable, "fact based" business enterprise is utterly natural."[17]

What's the point? The point is that we try to do ministry on our own strength and in our own power, instead of relying on God's divine intervention as we seek Him and pray.

Here's the right way. We find a positive example in this passage. The father in this passage also realizes he's in way over his head, just as disciples were. Is he self-confident? Not at all. He says to Jesus in verse 22, that if He can do anything, have compassion on them and help them, which implies that he's not even sure that Jesus can help him, and by this we know that he's not someone who has it all together.

Now, the problem is that we think Jesus only deals with people who have it all together. But it's the opposite: Jesus gives grace to those who acknowledge their need. When Jesus challenges him, the father says, "I believe; help my unbelief!" (Mark 9:24). Do you realize what he's saying? He is saying, "Help me just as I am, a doubter." He does not plead based on how together he is. He realizes that he has nothing to make himself worthy. He doesn't say, "Please heal my son based on how much faith I have!" Instead, he pleads for mercy and throws himself at Jesus' feet. As James Edwards said in his commentary on the book of Mark, *"True faith is always aware how small and inadequate it is."*[18]

There's a hint in this passage of how important this is. Mark has been drawing parallels between an Old Testament passage when Moses went up the mountain and met with God. Do you remember what Moses found when he came down from the mountain? He found the Israelites worshiping a golden calf. Here, Jesus has come down from the mountain after meeting with God. Do you see what he found? *Prayerless ministry.* Do you see what Mark is saying here? Prayerless ministry is no better than idolatry. It's putting our trust in technique and human strength instead of trusting in God alone.

Friends, this passage shows us that we have a tendency that is very dangerous. And if we persist in this tendency, we will never be able to serve as representatives of Jesus and plant a church that truly glorifies and honors our Lord, Jesus Christ. We will do ministry but it will lack power. The danger is that we will be self-reliant.

Henri Nouwen wrote:

We have fallen into the temptation of separating ministry from spirituality, service from prayer. Our demons say: "We are too busy to pray, we have too many needs to attend to, too many people to respond to, too many wounds to heal." Prayer is a luxury, something to do during a free hour, a day away from work or on a retreat.[19]

Perhaps we fear prayer, because, as Nouwen says,

Prayer is a way of being empty and useless in the presence of God and so proclaiming our basic belief that all is grace and nothing is simply the result of hard work.[20]

I'm convicted by this because I think it describes us pretty accurately. We are continually faced with situations in ministry that are greater than we can handle. The underdog church-planter needs to see that this passage reveals that we have a tendency to be self-reliant instead of God-reliant.

So here's the big question. What is the solution?

3. God calls us to repent and depend on Him for everything.

We see in this passage that God calls us to repent and depend on Him. This is not just a random story. This story is in the part of the Gospel of Mark that describes the preparation process. Jesus was preparing the disciples for future ministry, and they had to learn this lesson or else they could never carry out the mission that Jesus was going to entrust to them. It appears that they eventually learned because later on in Acts we see the disciples continually engaging in prayer.

What's the solution? First, we need to learn a lot from the father in this passage, and to admit to God that we believe, but we really don't. We accept that Jesus came to serve, to give his life, to rise so that we could have power and new life, but we still try to live on our own strength. Maybe right now what we need to do is repent, and even admit that we don't even know how to be dependent, and then ask God to help us. "I believe; help my unbelief!"

Second, Jesus said, "This kind can come out only by prayer." What challenges are you faced with as a minister of the gospel that can only be overcome by prayer?" When we encounter needs like the disciples did, where are we trying and arguing but not having any measurable impact? I wonder how things would change if we really believed what Jesus said in this passage; if we really acknowledged our need and depended on God for what only He can do.

Jack Miller was a pastor in Philadelphia. In 1970, Miller resigned from his church and seminary. Neither the church members nor the seminary students were changing in the ways that he had hoped. He didn't know how to help them, so he quit and spent weeks too depressed to do anything but cry. And he came to realize a couple of things: One, he was motivated by personal glory and the approval of people, rather than being motivated only by God's glory.

Two, he had been trusting in his own abilities, rather than in the promises God had made and the power of the Holy Spirit.

A turning point came when he realized his motivation for ministry had been all wrong, and that he had been relying on the wrong person to do ministry - himself. He came to understand that the work of ministry was far too big for him to accomplish on his own strength. He came to understand that it was his pride and self-reliance that was keeping him from having a significant part in this great work of Christ. He saw that doing Christ's work, in Christ's way, meant giving up all dependence on himself, acknowledging how poor in spirit he was, and then relying exclusively on Jesus and His gift of His Spirit.

He asked for his resignations back, and he changed. From that point on, his ministry was characterized by the themes of humility, vital faith, and constant prayer. He found that he grew as he admitted every day that he was "a desperate sinner in constant need of the grace of God". He believed that doing Christ's work, in Christ's way, is impossible using human resources; we must be connected to Christ through prayer. His ministry accomplished more than he could have thought once he got to the point of humble dependence instead of self-reliance.[21]

As underdog church-planters, we are continually faced with situations in ministry that are greater than we can handle. And yet we still have a tendency to be self-reliant instead of God-reliant. God calls us to repent and depend on him. Anything else is idolatry.

For Further Reflection

1. Do you remember the time when you were put in a position of responsibility that was way over your head?

2. Have you ever experienced in a situation in ministry where you felt overwhelmed because it's more than you can handle?

3. Why is the prayerless ministry no better than idolatry?

4. "I believe; help my unbelief" How will this prayer affect your ministry?

5. Where do you sense God wants you to be more dependent on Him?

the underdog church-planter as...
loving husband & father

Fabian Perea

"God has called you to lead, to lead with great joy and delight, to lead though it may be costly, and to lead with love. Lead your wife, lead your family, and do it all for the glory of God."

- Tim Challies

There are many challenges in the underdog church-planter's life. However, there are no doubts that being a loving husband and father is one of the most difficult to achieve. I have no doubt that even the enemy of God and of church planting is fighting to destroy our testimony and home and we cannot give him any advantage.

Even after 25 years being happily married to Marianela, raising two beautiful kids, Fabian Rafael (24) and Ana Karina (20), more than 27 years in the pastoral ministry and after having planted more than 14 churches, I have to confess that I still fight with myself to be the loving husband and father God wants me to be. I can say along with my mentor, the apostle Paul: "Not that I have already obtained this or am already perfect, but I press on to make it my own, because Christ Jesus has made me his own. But one thing I do: forgetting what lies behind and straining forward to what lies ahead, I press on toward the goal for the one prize of the upward call of God in Christ Jesus." (Philippians 3:12-14).

There are many ways of writing about this topic. I will break it down into seven bite-sized principles to consider both individually and as a whole. Josh McDowell defines a principle this way: "A principle is a norm or standard that may be applied to more than one type of situation... Principles help explain the 'why' behind a command."[22] In addition to this definition, I would like to add that a principle is an applied norm to any human being, in every culture, in every way. It is my prayer that the described principles here help you to be a loving husband and father as a servant of Jesus.

1. The Pastoral Principle

The underdog church-planter has to understand that family is the first ministry. There is a tension here. He has to minister to his family without losing his focus on planting churches or conversely using them as an excuse to not do the necessary labor of ministry.

Alex Strauch explains with detail in his book *Biblical Eldership* that the main tasks of the pastor are to: protect, nourish, guide and take care God's people.[23] We can approach Strauch's principles as applied to your family as well, if you believe your wife and children are an essential part of the flock that God has placed in your care.

If there is something that the modern church-planter must take care of it is this pastoral ministry to his family. For some reason we assume that they do not need our spiritual help or that someone else will fill this role. The truth is that if you do not, nobody else will. Your family has specific needs just as people in the town where God has called us to plant churches. They are not different. The fact of living in the same house does not mean they are not susceptible to sin, physical and emotional needs, problems and spiritual struggle, exactly as others.

In other words, I am saying that your first and unchanging church planting project is right there in your home. Your wife and children are the first ministry God has given you.

Practical Application
- **Counsel** based on the Word of God in every situation that arises.
- **Develop the "Family Altar"** at least once a week where the Word of God is read and meditated on. Share prayer requests and pray about 10 to 20 minutes as a family.
- **Relational Time:** Spend enough time engaging your family that you know any emotional and spiritual needs they have.
- **Wife / Children Coaching:** Make use of the elements of coaching with your wife and children.[24]

- **Family Prayer Time**: Set aside time to pray together as a family on a regular schedule.

2. The Intercession Principle

The only thing the disciples asked the Lord to teach them was to pray. Seriously! They did not request he teach them to cast out demons, or how to preach, or heal various diseases. The request was, "teach us to pray" (Luke 11: 1). Undoubtedly, this should also be the sincerest and most important request that an underdog church-planter brings to the Lord. A man who loves his family should be the first intercessor for them. He is the man who gets in the gap for his family (Ezekiel 22:30). The church-planter is the man who presents his family in holy and unceasing prayer before the Almighty, in particular, his marriage and his children. This means, it is not enough to pray only for our church planting project, but our most persistent prayers should be for our wives and our children.

Important Note: They must know that you are praying for them! I want insist with this: you should not assume that they know you are interceding for them. Tell them!

Practical Application

- **Passion in Prayer:** The prayers of a loving husband and father should be passionate and full of enthusiasm. It is not only a "ritual" before going to bed or before eating. To achieve this, use special words, leave the repetitive phrases out and be led by the Spirit.
- **Prayer Care:** Your family prayer is not the time to publicly expose the errors, weaknesses or failures of your family. Your prayers in front of them should be to highlight your love, care and passion for them.
- **Ask Them for Prayer Requests:** This not only lets you know your family's concerns, but shows them the spiritual interest you have for them.
- **Commitment:** Commit to pray daily and decidedly for their prayer requests.

3. The Principle of Example

Father God told his son: "You are my beloved Son, with you I am well pleased." (Luke 3:22). This is what I call the Example of Examples! We all need and want people who can be examples in our lives. The vast majority of us have people who we respect and admire. I think the reason is because their lifestyle impacts us so much that in the in the bottom of our hearts we want to be like them.

In a similar idea, Phil Downer says:

> As parents we are models to our children, Whether for good or bad. Parenting is modeling. Our children see us and follow our example, whether we like it or not. Men often say they do not want to be the spiritual leaders of their home, but I always respond that they are the spiritual leaders of their home, whether they like it or not. His desire (or lack of it) has nothing to do with it. The dad is the spiritual leader because God planned it that way. [25]

So what I really want to emphasize is that the influence of your example is powerful, undeniable and crucial to demonstrate God's love to your family and transform their lives.

The church-planter is the "ambassador" of God's love at home (2 Corinthians 5:20). Your challenge, but also your privilege, is that when they observe your life, they are able to see the clearest representation and practice of God's love on earth. You are the perfect candidate to demonstrate the love of God, not only to the lost, but to your family. No one else can be that kind of example.

Practical Application

- **Express Daily Gratitude:** You always have to say "thank you" to your wife and children when receiving a service or blessing from them. Always acknowledge what your wife does to look after you, your children and to serve God. Never stop saying "thank you."
- **Choose an Item from the Fruit of the Spirit (Gal. 5:22-23) Weekly:** Choose one of the fruits and try to carry it out during the week with practical actions.
- **Practice Generosity Monthly**: Let your family see how you can share with those in need from the blessings God has given you. Serve and

give regularly as an example and encourage your family to participate with you.

- **Reflect and Apply on Acceptance:** One of the most practical ways to do this is to meditate on how God has accepted you with all your sins, mistakes, weaknesses and evils. It sounds harsh, but God really knows you and knows who you are (as well as who I am). But even so, he has accepted us and has called us to be underdog church-planters!

- **Recognize and Observe Their Virtues:** Daily use words or phrases that affirm how you see God's grace at work in the lives of each family member. Pay attention to see their unique gifting and verbally affirm this until it become a habit.

4. The Reconciliation Principle

There will always be arguments with your spouse and children. However, in the heart of an underdog church-planter must be a willingness to be a "peacemaker" and find ways to reconcile.

Consider this as a special call for every servant of God, which the church-planter is not exempt: 2 Corinthians 5:20 says we are "ambassadors of Christ" to fulfill God's desire for peace between him and humanity and between human beings with other human beings. When reading this passage, it is easy to see that we are instruments of peace in God's hands.

There is no better place to practice the justice of forgiveness and the peace of reconciliation than at home in your marriage and parenting. The loving husband and father is a man who knows how to forgive, just as the Lord Jesus Christ taught in the vast, indescribable, and incomprehensible challenging work of the Cross.

Practical Application

- **Forgive as God the Father forgave you:** Remembering how God forgave us compels us to forgive our wife and children. He is our model of forgiveness.

- **Use the Scriptures:** Find and memorize key scriptures about forgiveness. They will help to promote forgiveness and reconciliation in your home.

- **"Do Not Let the Sun Go Down" (Ephesians 4:26):** Make it a goal to confront difficult situations right away. The sooner, the better.

5. The Impact Principle

At the time of writing these paragraphs, my brother and his son came to visit us. He was not a Christian, but something captivated his heart. He said, "you live like a real family." That's how we should all live." That was the perfect moment and place to explain that the merit was not from us but from our Lord Jesus Christ. He and only he had transformed and empowered us to live this way and to love one another.

In large part, it was the testimony of how we managed ourselves at home that captivated his attention. Just a couple of days later, his heart was ready to receive the message that has changed us so much, the gospel of Christ! Upon returning to his country, he told his family: "the gospel is beautiful."

The impact of your personal testimony not only will affect your own family, it will also impact believers and non-believers around you. I have wanted to differentiate this principle from the principle of the example. In which, we studied about the task of being examples of love for our spouse and children. But in this, my point is related to the impact of being a loving husband and father on your project of church planting. Being a man, husband and father full of God's love will be like a powerful light that attracts others to the feet of the transformer of lives, Jesus Christ.

Unfortunately, many ministers of the gospel have neglected this element. It can be said that they are light to the world, but darkness for their homes. Often this lack of love demonstrated in practical facts has impeded the lost world to put their faith in the transforming power of the gospel of Christ.

In fact, we need to recognize the argument of the non-believers is quite logical: *If this man is incapable of being transformed himself for the Gospel, how can he convince me of a real change in my own soul?* Is it strange to hear people giving an excuse for not believing the gospel due to these kind of bad testimonies? Not at all! Sometimes, we hear clear examples of ministers, pastors and missionaries who have fallen into sin and failed to be examples of love for their family or for themselves.

Definitely this is an excuse that the devil uses to distance the people from Christ. But also the impact of our testimony is vital to the development of our public ministry.

We must assume the importance of the principle from the point of view of Scripture. Paul exhorts, in almost all church planting projects to leaders and members to live and act according to the truth of the gospel. To the church in

Philippi he writes: "Only conduct yourselves in a manner worthy of the gospel of Christ" (Philippians 1:27). To the church in Colosse he writes, "so as to walk in a manner worthy of the Lord." (Colossians 1:10). He writes to the church in Thessalonica the following: "Finally, then, brothers , we ask and urge you in the Lord Jesus, that as you received from us how you ought to walk and to please God just as you are doing, that you do so more and more" (1 Thessalonians 4: 1).

However, there is a convicting passage for any man called by God to holy ministry, which includes the underdog church-planter. The Bible says: "I, therefore, a prisoner for the Lord, urge you to walk in a manner worthy of the calling to which you have been called." (Ephesians 4: 1). So everyone "called" by God must take care of their way of life, even and especially inside their home, to give the best testimony possible to those who live around them.

Practical application

- **Watch Your Public Behavior:** Develop a loving behavior toward your family outside your home both in your speech and actions.
- **Serve and Help Your Wife:** Especially with the work of caring for children whether in or out of the home, it's important to be involved in both the practical and spiritual raising of your children.

6. The Nutrition Principle

You get nutrients from food: vitamins, minerals, proteins, sugars and fats. They give you the energy required to move your muscles, activate your senses and even read the words on this page thanks to nutrients. However, not only the physical body must be fed but also the spirit. So, it is appropriate to ask ourselves: *where does the spiritual nourishment come for the underdog church-planter in order to feed our wife and children?*

This question makes us think about the source of that love. In the present age, the church-planter has many sources which could feed his soul and stimulate love and good works: parents, pastors, mentors, books, internet resources, conferences, and thousands more. But, the most important source of love is a person: the Holy Spirit. From your relationship with God, you will obtain the power to love as only God can love. The moment you lose sight of your dependence on God, your ability to love will also decrease.

The most important church-planter, the apostle Paul, said in Galatians 5:22 that the fruit of spirit is love. We extract from this passage that the producer and the inexhaustible source of love and other virtues is the Holy Spirit. The inexhaustible source of food and spiritual energy in your life is directly proportional to your relationship with God. That is why it is necessary to depend on his love, to feed from his love, to receive his love to obtain strength and energy, and perseverance to love your wife and your children unconditionally and selflessly.

Your relationship with God will enable you to understand the great, indescribable, challenging and incomprehensible love of Jesus on the cross. Loving. Forgiving. Redeeming. Yes! You can understand what cannot be understood, but only through the intervention of the Holy Spirit in your life. You truly love when you truly forgive.

There is a principle in education: you cannot teach what you haven´t learned. Or said another way, it is impossible to give something you haven´t received first. As you are nourished through the indwelling work of the Holy Spirit and begin to experience the fruit of the Spirit, you can now share this gift with your wife and children.

Practical application

- **Clamor Daily for Spiritual Food:** Being in God's Word is an integral part of your life and ministry. Do not neglect feeding your soul.
- **Accept Both Challenge**s**:** As you seek after God, I'm offering you two challenges. First, listen for the changes that God wants to make in you through his Word. Second, work alongside him and sacrifice yourself to obey.
- **Seek a Mentor or a Coach:** He will help you to share your challenge and progress in your relationship with the Holy Spirit's leading.

7. The Principle of "Turn Off"

I remember a conversation that was very funny to me some time ago. We were talking about physical exercise and muscle development. (You know, guy talk.) And suddenly one of the women in the room said: "By the way... Do you know what is the most developed muscle of my husband?" We all looked at each other in amazement and she told us: "The muscle of his thumb - The best machine for him to exercise is the TV remote control!"

The worst thing is we can add several items to our list of "Boys Toys." Ipads, laptops, cell phones, tools, and even our own car. We are in the "high tech" era, but, we can say without fear of contradiction that people have more technology but are less connected than ever. The reason is very simple: these devices take much time from us. Time we could devote to our family and to be in the presence of God is now spent staring at our screen of choice. I wonder how much time we spend on Facebook, Pokemon Go, Instagram, video games, YouTube, et cetera? (Have you considered keeping track?) In the same way, how much family time do we enjoy? This is not only a good reflection but a tremendous challenge for every loving husband and father. I understand the struggle this produces in men, BUT it's time to turn off the TV, the computer, the phone and the tablet.

Probably this principle is one of the most difficult to apply, because the temptation is near us every day and all the time. Our guy, the apostle Paul tells another man, who had no "Boys Toys": "making the best use of the time , because the days are evil" (Ephesians 5: 16). Any approach you make from this passage will take you to the exhortation of being a better manager of time that God gives you.

Practical application

- **Plan Your "Cyber -Time":** Consider what is a reasonable amount of time and ask someone to keep you accountable (you can download software or an app on your phone to help you too). Social media, email, and online games can be big time suckers.
- **Turn Off the Phone:** Naturally, you can't do this all the time, but always during meals and, if possible, for large chunks of time on the weekends.
- **Set "Office Hours":** Try not bringing your work to your home, although I know for some church-planters, a lot of our work happens at home. Consider establishing work hours that don't detract from time with the family.
- **Do Not Answer the Cell Phone:** Related to the point above, do not answer calls concerning work outside of the "office hours." especially when you are at home. This can be difficult, and naturally you must be

discerning based on circumstances and concerns in the church body, but you have the responsibility to set these boundaries for the sake of leading and loving your family.

For Further Reflection

1. What are two principles you find compelling that you are not using right now?

2. What would be the plan of action to start using them?

3. Do you have a mentor or coach with whom you could discuss your personal advancement in application of these principles?

the underdog church-planter as...
persistent prayer

Mark Hallock

"Some people think God does not like to be troubled with our constant coming and asking. The way to trouble God is not to come at all."

- D.L. Moody

Before coming to Calvary seven years ago, I served as a youth pastor for many years. I believed in the power of prayer, no question. I believed that in ministry we need the power of God to move in the hearts of people in order to see lives truly transformed for His glory. But I can tell you, it wasn't until God called me to Calvary to be part of seeing new churches planted and dying churches replanted that I became desperate for God in prayer. For a while in ministry, you might be able to lean on your own gifting and passion and zeal. But when you're looking at a situation where God has to show up in power or "this isn't going to go," (as is the case in church planting), you don't understand how deep your need for prayer really is. The Lord has continued to make me see and feel my need for surrendered, desperate, persistent prayer. This is His grace at work. I'm convinced more than ever that persistent prayer has been and always will be the most important discipline and practice for the Underdog Church-Planter.

Several years ago, a friend introduced me to a book by an old Methodist-Episcopal pastor named E.M. Bounds. He wrote a book in 1913 called *Power through Prayer*. This was a profound book for me as I hadn't before read a book that was so zealous for prayer in the life of every believer. The implications of Bound's book were massive, not only for my life with God, but for my ministry. There's a particular paragraph from the book that has stuck with me for years.

I come back to this short paragraph regularly to be reminded and convicted of my deep need for persistent prayer. Bounds says:

> "What the Church needs today is not more machinery or better, not new organizations or more and novel methods, but men whom the Holy Ghost can use – men of prayer, men mighty in prayer. The Holy Ghost does not flow through methods, but through men. He does not come on machinery, but on men. He does not anoint plans, but men – men of prayer."[26]

When I first read this paragraph I thought, "God, make me that kind of man. Make me the kind of pastor that's on fire for you and your purposes by your Holy Spirit, because of prayer. Make me prayerfully dependent on you in all things." I became convinced that this kind of prayer is needed in all churches, and particularly in church plants. If God is going to move, if God is going to bring the spiritually dead back to life, if God is going to breathe life and zeal into towns and communities through new church plants, then we need men that are going to fall on their face in prayer. But here's the thing, it's not only that Underdog Church-Planters must be men of prayer, but priority #1 must be that they lead church plants where prayer is central. Churches made up of praying people.

I often think of a story that I heard years ago about Charles Spurgeon. There was a group of American pastors who went over to London because they had heard of the great Spurgeon. They heard about this Baptist preacher; how his church was blowing up; and how they were reaching thousands upon thousands of lost people with the Gospel. So this group of American pastors are over there asking, "What's the secret? We've got to see this for ourselves." They visit Spurgeon and his church. Spurgeon takes them for a walk through the church building. It's a Sunday morning, the time of morning when worship is going on. Folks are singing in the sanctuary. He takes these pastors into the depths of the church building … into the boiler room. Spurgeon opens the door and all of a sudden, in front of them is a group of four hundred people on their knees praying; Praying for the service, praying that God would move in power, praying for Spurgeon as a preacher. Spurgeon then looks as this group of men and says, "There, gentlemen, there is the secret for God's blessing His work here."

I remember hearing that story and thinking, "Our church *must* have prayer like that because we *need* God to move like that!" It is through prayer that the power of God moves in and transforms the hearts of people. For this reason, one of the first things that we must prioritize in our lives and in our church plants is this kind of devoted, dependent, persistent prayer.

When we go to the Scriptures, one example of an underdog church-planter who believed in the power of prayer was the Apostle Paul. He was a man passionate about prayer and we see this throughout his letters. Here are just a few examples.

In Romans 15:30, he writes:

"I appeal to you, brothers, by our Lord Jesus Christ and by the love of the Spirit, to strive together with me in your prayers to God on my behalf…"

This "striving" is almost a sense of fighting together in prayer! Paul understood the battle he was in. "Oh, I need your prayers! Strive together with me, fight together with me in prayer! For this ministry, for these people!"

In Ephesians 6:18-20, Paul here is unapologetically asking the Christians in Ephesus to pray for him:

"…at all times in the Spirit, with all prayer and supplication. To that end keep alert with all perseverance, making supplication for all the saints, and also for me, that words may be given to me in opening my mouth boldly to proclaim the mystery of the Gospel, for which I am an ambassador in chains, that I may declare it boldly, as I ought to speak."

With Paul, in our church planting efforts, prayer must be a top priority. Let me share twelve specific ways Underdog Church-Planters must pray for our lives and ministries. These are twelve key areas in which not only we as individuals need to be praying, but also our church members.

1. Pray we will keep our eyes on God and not take a step apart from God's leading.

In church planting, we can quickly mess things up! Am I right? I know this has been so true in my own life and ministry; Mistakes and poor choices I've made as a leader as a result of following my own lead instead of the Lord's. We must crave a constant, humble dependence that keeps our eyes focused on God. Let our constant plea be: "Oh Lord! Don't let me take one wrong step. Let me be in line with you and keep in step with your Spirit."

2. Pray for courage and boldness to go where the Lord leads.

As the Lord leads us, as the Lord leads our congregations, we need to pray for courage and boldness. Some of us need to grow in our courage as leaders. (Psalm 31:24) We need to grow in our boldness because ministry can be scary. People can be "scary" and our fear of them can cause us to become overly timid in our leadership. Yet, the Lord has called to us to lead and to pastor by His grace and in His power. Because of this, we pray for courage and we pray for boldness to go where the Lord is leading, even in the face of criticism and opposition.

3. Pray for humility before the Lord and people, prioritizing the raising up of other leaders.

Humility must be our constant posture in prayer before God. Our egos must be kept in check. We must constantly pray that our pride would not get in the way of the Lord's work in our lives and in our churches… That we would stay humble before the Lord. (James 4:10) Ask God daily, "Make me humble before your people."

I think one of the ways that we practice this kind of humility is through the prioritization of praying for God to raise up other leaders. It's one thing to pray for humility. It is another to lead from a place of humility alongside others. One of the action steps we must take to help see this become a reality is to raise up others to lead alongside you. This is one of many reasons why a plurality of pastor-elders is so critical to our leadership effectiveness in the local church. So we pray: "Lord, raise up other leaders. Raise up other men who can help shepherd this church. It's not all about me. I don't want to make this all about me. This church will never get to be as healthy as you want it to be if it's just me trying to do this thing. So God, please raise up leaders who can shepherd the flock."

4. Pray we will not rely on our own strength, but trust in the Lord's strength.

One of my favorite hymns is "I Need Thee Every Hour." The chorus of this great hymn should be one that we sing every day to the Lord: "*Lord I need Thee, oh I need Thee. Every hour I need Thee. O bless me now my Savior, I come to Thee.*" If we ever move beyond a dependent posture of prayer, we're in big trouble. We cannot rely on our own strength in church planting. We might be able to pull it off for a while, but ultimately this will lead us to discouragement, burn-out, or worse. When we are seeking to do ministry in our own strength, things go south fast. Our walk with the Lord suffers. Our marriages suffer. Our preaching is weak. Our leadership is poor. Our hearts are cold. So we pray, "Oh God, help me not to rely on my own strength but to be totally reliant on Your strength."

5. Pray for love in leading God's people.

What do our people need more than anything else from us? They need love. They need to know we care about them. They need to hear it, see it and feel it. Do they know we love them? Do we tell them? Do we show them? Do they feel it? Do they hear it? Do they see it? And so we pray, "Lord, fill me with Your love for Your people. Empower me to joyfully and sacrificially love your sons and daughters that are under my care."

6. Pray for the health of our wives, marriages, and families.

If we aren't doing the job we need to do at home to shepherd our wives and our families, then we've got no business shepherding the flock of God. That's a harsh, hard truth. If we're going to be the type of men, the leaders that God has called us to be in the church, we must understand the seriousness of this. "Lord, help me do whatever it takes to love my wife. To love my kids. To lead and shepherd my family well by your power. May this increasingly be my #1 priority and passion in life."

May we commit ourselves to be prayer warriors for our families. We should pray specifically for our wives' relationship with the Lord. There's nothing worse for a pastor than when your wife is not growing in the Lord. It is hard on you. It is hard on your family. In contrast, when your wife is growing in the Lord, it gives you joy! This is what we want for her and for our family. We must do whatever it takes to help our wives and our kids grow closer to Jesus.

7. Pray we will walk worthy of the calling God has placed on our lives.

Each of us must be regularly reminded of Paul's words in Colossians 1:

"We haven't stopped praying for you . . . so that you may walk worthy of the Lord, fully pleasing to Him, bearing fruit in every good work and growing in the knowledge of God." (Col. 1:9-10)

The Lord has called us to this work. The Lord has chosen us for this work. And so humbly we ask, "Oh God, help us to walk worthy of this calling in the power of your Spirit."

8. Pray we will preach the Word and the Gospel boldly.

The Gospel offends. It just does. If we're going to be preachers of the Word, we must be ready to offend with the Gospel. Yet, it's that very Gospel that also takes dead people and makes them alive. It's the same Gospel that saved you and saved me by God's grace. "Lord give us boldness in the pulpit. In the face of challenges in our culture and in the face of challenges in this church, help me to be bold. Help me to be clear in my preaching of your Word… because your Word is what changes people's hearts." May we echo the words of Paul who wrote from a prison cell in Ephesians 6:

"Pray also for me, that the message may be given to me when I open my mouth to make known with boldness the mystery of the Gospel." (Ephesians 6:19)

9. Pray for God to destroy idols in our hearts and in the hearts of our people.

John Calvin said: "Our hearts are idol-making factories." It's true. We are so quick to worship things other than God. We set up idols in our hearts in place of Jesus. And so, we must pray that God will destroy idols in our hearts and in the hearts of our people. Each of us need His help to identify the things we are worshiping instead of Jesus and ask God, by His grace, to destroy these idols through the preached word, through prayer, and through the power of the Spirit. It's these idols that often get in the way of our growth in holiness and sanctification. This is true in our own hearts as pastors and it's true in the hearts of the people in our congregations.

10. Pray for a renewed sacrificial love for others that leads to God-honoring unity.

Unity. In church planting, it is critical to do whatever it takes to pursue unity. We love our people and we pray for unity. We must strive to do the best we can to wave the banner of true, loving unity in our churches. We do this because there's nothing more powerful and God-glorifying than a church that is unified in love, being led by the Spirit of God. I'm convinced of that. Of course, Satan hates unity and seeks to bring division whenever and however he can. We must fight for unity. And the most effective way to fight is on our knees in prayer. This is hard work we must do as Underdog Church-Planters: Praying for unity and wisdom to lead well, so that this kind of Christ-exalting unity becomes a reality.

11. Pray we will do whatever it takes to reach the lost.

Sadly, for many pastors, the longer he serves in the church, the easier it gets to become numb to the lost. It is easy to become desensitized to the reality that those apart from Christ are on their way to an eternity spent separated from Him. This should break our hearts. So we plead in prayer: "Oh God, break our hearts every time we go to the grocery store that there are people who don't know you and may I do whatever it takes; may we do whatever it takes to reach them." Let's pray fervently, "Oh Lord, make my heart sensitive to those far from you. May the reality of knowing they will spend an eternity separated from you if they do not come to know Christ break my heart and move me to action!"

Of course, this is a huge challenge, which is why only through prayer can it happen. We can preach and instruct about why we need to evangelize and why we need to reach the lost, but I'm convinced that it's only through prayer that a heart of stone becomes a heart of flesh. (Ezekiel 36:26) And that's what has to happen in and through our churches! Not only must my heart break for the lost, but the hearts of the people sitting in my congregation must break as well. Only then will we be willing to do whatever it takes to actually reach the lost with the Gospel. We need God. "Oh Lord, move in power! Help us to be outward focused not inward focused. Make us a people who are passionate to lay down our idols in order to reach the lost. Break our hearts over the things that break Your heart."

12. Pray for the making of disciples who make disciples in and through our church plant.

We have been called by Jesus to go show and tell the Gospel boldly… To make disciples of all nations, baptizing them in the name of the Father, and the Son, and the Holy Spirit, teaching them to obey everything that Jesus commanded. (Matthew 28:19-20) This means we're not interested in just making a few disciples and planting one church. We want to see, by God's grace, a mass movement of God planting hundreds and thousands of churches for His glory! Churches where the lost are being saved and disciples are being made! As we pray for the lost to come to Christ, we pray they would see that they have been called to be disciple-makers themselves. We pray these believers would see that as Christ-followers, we have all been sent out on mission, and what a joy it is! This is what our cities need. It is what our country needs. It's what our world needs. Join with me and fervently pray the Lord makes this happen so that His fame will spread to the ends of the earth.

For Further Reflection

1. *Where is your prayer life strongest right now? Where is it weakest?*

2. *What is one step you could take to improve your personal prayer life?*

3. *How can you encourage your leaders and those in your congregation to prioritize prayer in their own lives?*

4. *What Scripture will you cling to as you strive to make prayer central to your Underdog Church Planting?*

5. *Is there someone you know who is a "prayer warrior" who you can ask to pray for you? Do it today!*

practices
of the underdog church-planter

the underdog church-planter as...
humble leader

Jim Misloski

"Humility is the displacement of self by the enthronement of God."

- **Andrew Murray**

It happened midway into his second year of vocational ministry. He was sorting through the daily mail at home. He had stopped to study an envelope from a member who served on a ministry team he led. This leader's team met weekly and a letter in the mail was cause for curiosity. Curiosity turned to devastation as soon as the letter unfolded. Vicious words jumped off the pages and clawed the young pastor's senses. It was an angry resignation letter. There had been no warning signs for this kind of letter. The team member was outstanding and their exchanges had been positive and productive. She was part of a motivated team leading his church to multiply disciples through Bible study groups at a healthy, God-glorifying pace.

A phone call to the team member let her know her resignation had been received. The young pastor asked if she would be willing to meet at church at her convenience along with someone she trusted. She chose one of his deacons and all three of them sat down together. The deacon was unaware of the letter. The pastor listened and asked questions but desperately wanted to vent and defend himself. Though he had discarded the letter he now wanted it to come through the door of their meeting room and convict his team member of her unrighteousness and vindicate him. She aired her grievances and hurts. The deacon patiently observed the exchange and gave the young leader some suggestions for leading his team and this member more effectively going forward.

Sitting in his chair receiving correction and listening while everything in him wanted to defend his reputation as a leader was taking its toll. He was tired. Quietly though, another voice began to speak. The Spirit slowly helped him understand this meeting was not about him and his reputation as a leader. He began to notice this person across from him was wearier than he was. She needed to vent. She needed to express resentments from the past that had been building up pressure without release. These feelings needed to come out in a safe place where she would be heard and not judged. His team member needed to express her needs and be understood and acknowledged. The postural change that came over him during this meeting was a transformational move of God in his soul. There was no other explanation.

That young pastor has grown to become the author of this chapter. Only the Jesus who was falsely accused, judged, and torn apart on the cross, and yet continued to love the people who initiated the torture, could suggest the path He led me on that day. He had graciously allowed me to taste a sip of the humiliation He guzzled for us on the cross. Unlike Jesus, I was not completely innocent as a leader in this person's life. I cannot come close to understanding His suffering. And yet, it was enough for me to begin to understand words like those of Paul: "That I may know him and the power of his resurrection, and may share his sufferings, becoming like him in his death…"[27]

Because of the Spirit's guidance in our meeting, I experienced the power of humility as a growing shepherd of God's people. More importantly, our wounded team member did not resign. Continuing on to serve our team well, she eventually joined the core team of a church plant sent out by our church and continues in even greater service in the kingdom.

The Fountain of Humility

Our original break from the Heavenly Father was initiated by our lack of humility. Pride is our flaw. Jesus' humbled himself before His Father on the cross to reverse the pride we exhibited in the garden. The humble underdog church-planter knows that if he wants to drink from the fountain of humility he must go to the cross. Paul's invitation for us to drink from this fountain is clear.

> Have this mind among yourselves, which is yours in Christ Jesus, who, though he was in the form of God, did not count equality with God a thing to be grasped, but emptied himself, by taking the form of a servant, being born in the likeness

of men. And being found in human form, he humbled himself by becoming obedient to the point of death, even death on a cross.[28]

Even before Jesus completed His work on the cross, God graciously employed Isaiah to make this fountain available to leaders of his day in the book of Isaiah. I believe the following messianic preview of Jesus gives us a glimpse into the mindset Paul encourages us to have in Philippians 2.

The Lord God has given me the tongue of those who are taught, that I may know how to sustain with a word him who is weary. Morning by morning he awakens; he awakens my ear to hear as those who are taught. The Lord God has opened my ear, and I was not rebellious; I turned not backward. I gave my back to those who strike, and my cheeks to those who pull out the beard; I hid not my face from disgrace and spitting. But the Lord God helps me; therefore I have not been disgraced; therefore I have set my face like a flint, and I know that I shall not be put to shame. He who vindicates me is near. Who will contend with me? Let us stand up together. Who is my adversary? Let him come near to me. Behold, the Lord God helps me; who will declare me guilty? Behold, all of them will wear out like a garment; the moth will eat them up.[29]

Four Principles to Guide the Humble Leader

At least four principles fall out of this passage that help the underdog church-planter find and remain on the path of humility Jesus blazed for us.

Principle #1: Sustaining the Weary with a Word

Verse four of our Isaiah passage establishes the essential work of a humble church-planter. It is the work of sustaining with a word those who are weary. In the book of Luke when the disciples asked Jesus to teach them to pray, he told them a story about man who had a friend on a journey who had come to him. This man had nothing to give this friend and out of necessity approaches his neighbor to ask for three loaves of bread. In spite of his neighbor's protests he finally produces the badly needed bread. Jesus sums up the story of the asking-for-bread man by saying: "…how much more will the heavenly Father give the Holy Spirit to those who ask him!"[30]

Through this story, Jesus is explaining what He meant by teaching the disciples to ask for daily bread. As underdog church-planters, we are the asking-for-bread man in the story. We have people coming to us on a journey every weekend. If you're a dad, you have children coming to you everyday. They are on a journey. If you're a husband, you have a wife that is coming to you on a journey. If you have church members, friends, co-workers, employees, or neighbors, all of them are coming to you on their journey. Like the man in Jesus' story, we don't have anything to give them. We think we do, and in thinking so make a fatal error. We often attempt to sustain the weary with our strengths and gifts and talents and gallant acts of service. These may comfort for a time, but they will never substitute for deeply satisfying, life-giving truths found in Jesus' life and the Word that reveals Him. The humble church-planter, like the asking-for-bread man, has come to the realization that he brings nothing to the table. He has stopped putting confidence in the flesh. He no longer trusts his own ability to manufacture the bread of heaven. He knows he must get them directly from the Lord and he must go there daily. Verse four says, "Morning by morning He awakens my ear like those who are being taught."[31] (Isa. 50:4)[5] This humble leader acknowledges the same posture of those he is leading. He is going to Lord daily for bread he desperately needs himself, and bread to share with the weary. And like the manna in the wilderness, it's only good for each day. Daily dependence on the presence of God for everything is an essential premise of humility revealed in this passage. Progressive growth in humility is a growing more and more dependent on the sustaining, life-giving presence of God.

Notice in Isaiah 50:4-9 how much of the work the leader attributes to the Lord. The Lord gives the tongue, the Lord wakes the ear, the Lord opens the ear, the Lord helps, the Lord vindicates, and the Lord declares me innocent. According this leader, all of the heavy lifting is being done by the Lord. The humble leader believes that the God who called him to minister is actively engaged in the work of his ministry. The underdog church-planter must be aware and conscious of how completely dependent he is on all the Lord is providing to allow him to bring a welcome word to weary people.

In the asking-for-bread story, the man is not asking for himself alone. He is asking for enough bread to share with others who are on a journey. Jesus, in the Lord's prayer (Luke 11), is teaching us to ask Him for not just enough bread for ourselves, but bread to share.

Most Christian leaders like this part of the call to ministry. The call to feed and lead the weary with a word is deeply satisfying to shepherds. What is not so satisfying is to remain in the knowledge that we are as needy and as weary as those we are called to shepherd. Henri Nouwen, in his book *The Wounded Healer* tells an ancient Jewish parable of a prophet looking for the messiah. The prophet is told he will find the messiah sitting among the lepers. In addition, the prophet is told he will recognize the messiah because of the way he bandages his sores differently than the other lepers.[32] The humble church-planter remembers that even as one called to lead, the only difference between him and the flock is how he cares for his own wounds.

Principle #2: Beard Pulling and Back Beating Are Part of the Job Description

Jesus offered His beard to be plucked and his back to be beaten. It is crucial the humble underdog church-planter understand what the call to ministry really means. Weary, hurting people take it out on others. Our greatest hurts and wounds in ministry will come from the hands of the disciples we love and serve under our own "steeples." They less often come from un-regenerated souls outside of the church. The delusions of a young pastor quickly evaporate in the face of messy, Christian people who lash out at their shepherds. Isaiah writes that the leader in this passage was not rebellious and did not turn back but gave his beard and back to those who would strike him. The church-planter must understand the call to take a beating and not strike back or shrink back, but to lean in to hurting people and create safe space for them to work out their pain and suffering.

Identifying the real enemy during these times is critical. We must set realistic expectations if we want to develop proper responses to the difficulties ministry will present the underdog church-planter. Those we are called to sustain, to love, to serve and to equip are not our enemies. We have a real enemy who often presents himself through flesh and blood people. In the midst of battle, we must fight to focus on who is friend and who is foe if we're going to respond rightly to both. In the midst of these times, the reputation of the leader will be challenged or maligned. The humble church-planter understands during these seasons that effectiveness is not about his reputation; it is about God's reputation. If we will be faithful to focus on His renown, God will be faithful to defend our reputation in His timing. Being understood as leader is a luxury, not a right. Jesus was not always understood and often He did not spend time explaining Himself. You will be opposed. You will be questioned. You will be doubted. Do not avoid or hide from these challenges.

Lean into them and love those who are landing the blows. Most often there is a weary, hurting individual behind them that needs someone with courage to lead them to life in Christ by enduring their punches.

In every Rocky movie there is a similar scene. After Rocky Balboa has been severely beaten and it appears he has lost the fight, some turn of events inspires him. At that point in the movie he gets back up to fight and surprisingly drops his hands, sticks his jaw out and invites his opponent to hit him as hard as he can. He has come to realize there is something inside of him that can't be defeated. It makes for a great movie. But it makes for even greater ministry moments. We must not shrink back from the blows delivered by the people we are shepherding. They are not fatal if we are indwelt by the overcomer. Jesus promises us, "In this world you will have trouble but fear not for I have overcome the world."[33] The full weight of our confidence can be put on this promise.

Principle #3: Developing A Face Like Flint

Rocky Balboa's stone jaw doesn't compare to the face of flint Jesus portrayed in scripture. Both Isaiah 50:7 and Luke 9:51 reflect this image of Jesus resolutely setting and keeping His sights focused on His mission to get to Jerusalem and the cross to save us. Scripture does not offer a passive, weak view of humility in its leaders.

It should be no surprise then that our best leadership thinkers agree there is a certain kind of humble confidence found in our most effective leaders. *Good to Great* author Jim Collins defines a "Level 5" leader as one who, "builds enduring greatness through a paradoxical blend of personal humility and professional will."[34] Jeanine Prime and Elizabeth Salib, in the *Harvard Business Review* (2014), confirm what Collins has reported. Taken all together, existing research confirms that these leaders who are able to combine humility with determination really are the best leaders.[35]

The question of how these seemingly opposing characteristics come together in one person is an important question for the underdog church-planter. Humility and confidence are not competing opposites as many have proposed. Humility and arrogance are the real opposites. It has been said arrogance is misplaced confidence. Humility then is the art of learning to exercise confidence in the right places. Humility and arrogance are actually the by-products of where we place our confidence. If we place our confidence in the Lord, we will cultivate humility. If we place our confidence in our abilities, we will cultivate arrogance. The leader in Isaiah 50:4-9 gives us a great picture of what it looks like to place our confidence in the Lord and the confident humility that grows out of properly placed confidence. Where does this confidence in the Lord get forged?

Throughout scripture we observe a pattern. It seems as though the Lord calls a ministry leader long before He sends them. "He equips the called, He doesn't call the equipped," is a phrase you may have heard, and it refers to this biblical pattern. Moses is called to deliver Israel yet spends 40 years caring for livestock in the desert. David is anointed as king long before he takes the throne and must shepherd and fight for years before doing so. Jesus labors as a carpenter years before he launches his three-year mission to the cross. The fierce humility we observe in these biblical leaders appears to be forged in apprenticeship type seasons *after* hearing the Lord call them to the vision. Humble church-planters will do well to note the difference between the call and the send, and humbly submit themselves to whatever work the Lord gives their hands in the place between the call and the send.

Principle #4: Humility is the Key to Sustainability

Isaiah's passage called the humble leader to sustain the weary with a word. Ironically, the passage leaves us with a humble leader who has been sustained in the face of the forces that have conspired against him. In contrast to this picture, most statistics reflect that 60% to 80% of those who enter the ministry will not be serving 10 years later, and only a fraction will stay in ministry as a lifetime career.[136] The leader in our passage is sustained not because he didn't experience the troubles and trials that eliminated others. He has been plucked and beaten. He has been disgraced and spit upon. He has faced the enemy in battle. Our leader has lasted because of his fierce, humble, dependence on the Lord. The green willow survives the storm when the mighty oak does not because it is designed to bend low in the face of storm and the oak is not.

Conclusion

In the storms of ministry, the underdog church-planter will face confusion regarding the size of God and the size of man. This is often the cause of our fall. Is your God big enough? Can He really create and sustain this vast, enormous universe and at the same time number the hairs on the head of every man, woman and child on the earth? Does He really care about you? Did He really knit you in your mother's womb and lay out your days before you were born? Is He really aware of the detail of your life today and the challenges you are facing as one of his children? Will He really come through for you as you place your confidence in His ability and willingness to prevail?

And is your man small enough? Are you more concerned with defending Jesus' reputation than you are defending your own? Are you comfortable in a story where you are not the central character? Are you comfortable serving as an extra to the real star of the show or do you constantly find yourself photobombing Jesus? The humble underdog church-planter is one who can properly discern the size of his God and the size of his man. He is the one who will find the path to sustainability and joy in his service to the Lord.

For Further Reflection

1. Describe, in your own words, what it means for you to have the same attitude as Christ Jesus.

2. Jesus set his face like flint toward Jerusalem. What is the mission or the vision that God called you to "set your face like flint" toward?

3. How do the sufferings in your life train you to be obedient (see Hebrews 5:8-10)?

4. Describe a time when you "offered your beard to be plucked and your back to be beaten." What did you learn through the experience?

5. Jesus had the power of God, yet He stooped to wash His disciples' feet. What opportunities do you have to demonstrate similar humility?

6. If you drew a map of where you currently place your confidence what would it look like?

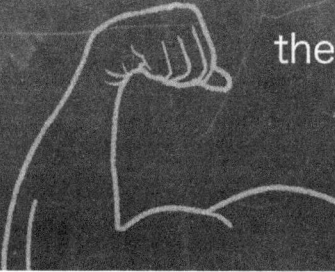

the underdog church-planter as...
joyful shepherd

Steve Anderson

"Because you are a present partaker in the glory to be revealed, a future partaker in the crown of glory, and a beneficiary of God's total saving dominion, you are free and empowered to shepherd the flock of God among you."

- Jared Wilson

I heard a well-known pastor speak recently. If I told you his name you may recognize it. As he began, he quickly captivated the room with humor, quick speech, and a sharp wit. For the 45 minutes he spoke, he had my attention. Indeed, I felt like I didn't want to miss whatever was coming next.

When his sermon was finished, I left reflecting on what I had just heard. Walking through hallways and parking lots of the church I was visiting, reflecting on this pastor and his message, I quickly realized what clearly stood out in my mind were the outrageous stories he shared and his off-the-cuff humor—but his main points were lost to me. Forty-five minutes of preaching about the Bible, and I could barely recall what he had just said. And I value listening to sermons. I'm a pastor!

This experience reminded me of a few things. It reminded me that funny communication does not necessarily mean clear communication. It reminded me of the importance of an outline. But deeper and more profound than either of these, I was reminded that in American Christian culture there is not a clear answer to the question, *what is a pastor?* And if there is one thing an underdog church-planter must be, it is a faithful pastor.

So, again, what exactly is a pastor? What does a pastor do? What should you expect from a pastor? If you were to ask a variety of people these questions, you no doubt would get a variety of answers depending on experience, church background, theology, etc. What should a pastor be like? What's the right skill set? What separates good pastors from bad pastors?

I am going to argue that the Bible clearly answers the question, *what is a pastor?* We will look at the evidence in this chapter. But first, I want to consider the American church landscape and what it has to say. With a brief survey, we see there are several popular models.

Popular Pastoral Models

The CEO

The CEO-pastor is the leader of leaders. He is the captain of the ship and the primary (if not sole) leader in the minds of the congregation. He runs the church like a business, organizes the church like a corporation, and employs the best leadership knowledge of the business world to inform his decisions and his role. When someone asks, "who's your pastor"—even if the church is 15,000 people—everyone points to him. In this model, the pastor is a professional and his job is running the church.

The Entertainer

The Entertainer-pastor is the pastor that everyone loves watching and listening to. He is funny and likable, he is visually appealing, and church members want their friends to come and hear him. You never know what will be on the stage during a service, or what he will come up with next. He teaches the Bible, though it may be a little lost in the show, and his sermons sure are fun! He draws a crowd and they leave happy. He always keeps your attention and his church is kept entertained.

The Activist

The Activist-pastor lives in the realm of social change. The primary goal is seeing the church "make a difference," and he leads the church to do this in the community and around the world. He knows the local politicians and non-profit leaders. Church life is built around supporting causes and getting involved. His preaching focuses on social and community issues and leads congregants to do something, make a difference, and get involved in the community.

The Therapist

The Therapist-pastor is a self-help guru with a Christian twist. Like the church's very own Dr. Phil he is insightful and well-spoken, and he seems to know what to do in any situation. He may use the Bible in his teaching and counseling, but he's known for his phrase, "all truth is God's truth." The advice is clever and helpful, and it "works," so there's no reason to question it. Sermons consist of helpful principles from the Bible, or just from life, that God gave us to make our lives better.

The Cool Guy

The Cool Guy-pastor is trendy, relevant, and gets the culture. His main function is being a role model. In attempts to be culturally relevant (or "not weird") he dresses with the latest trends, may be a self-proclaimed beer snob, and has a prominent social media presence. He went to seminary, but doesn't really use that stuff anymore. His "work week" consists of hanging out with people and diving deeper into hobbies so that people can see what it means to be "real." Some people say he seems like just an average guy and not very Christian-y. But for the Cool Guy-pastor, that is mission accomplished.

Now these are clearly caricatures, and my intention is not to throw stones at pastors, churches, or traditions. There are plenty of churches not like ours who are doing awesome things for the Kingdom of God. Neither is my intention to say that everything in each of these models is bad. There are helpful practices to glean from each one. And, I expect that any pastor would read these descriptions and be convicted by parts of themselves they see in at least a couple—I know I am!

However, I do hope to illustrate two things. First, and as I said above, there is no single understanding of who a pastor is or what he should do. Second, each of these models—which I would venture to say represent the vast majority of growing churches in our country—is anemic. Each of these should leave us wanting more in the leadership of our churches. And my prayer is that for the underdog church-planter called by God to serve the church in this specially ordained way, you are left yearning for more—for something richer and more amazing—than any of these models provides.

So I would like to present an alternative model that I believe is explicitly clear in scripture, and which we will spend the rest of this chapter unpacking:

The Pastor as Joyful Shepherd. We will first consider the biblical grounds, and then consider the practical application.

The Heart of God in Psalm 23

Shepherding imagery is plentiful in scripture in both the Old and New Testaments. In Genesis, we see Israel refer to Yahweh as "the God who has been my shepherd all my life" (Gen. 48:15). In the oft-quoted introduction to Psalm 23, we read, "The Lord is my shepherd." The author of Psalm 95 refers to Israel as "the people of [God's] pasture, the flock under his care" (Ps. 95:7) and Jesus sends the disciples to "the lost sheep of Israel" (Matt. 10:6). Jesus also refers to himself as "the good shepherd" (Jn. 10:11). To the extent that Jesus was a shepherd, his disciples ought also to be shepherds, and we see this precedent found in Jesus' Great Commission. More specifically, we see Paul addressing the elders of Ephesus, saying, "Keep watch over yourselves and all the flock of which the Holy Spirit has made you overseers. Be shepherds of the church of God, which he bought with his own blood" (Acts 20:28). Likewise, Peter addresses the elders among his readers, exhorting them to "be shepherds of God's flock that is under your care" (1 Pet. 5:2). It quickly becomes clear that the heart of God is the heart of a shepherd.

Examples are abundant, yet there is none that more clearly shows the shepherd heart of God than Psalm 23. This psalm describes the confidence the believer can have in the Lord because of his shepherding care and love. Additionally, in this Psalm we see the four functions of Biblical shepherding.[37]

Knowing the Sheep

Psalm 23 paints a picture of the way God loves His people, like a shepherd who cares deeply for his sheep. This can only occur when the shepherd knows the sheep. The rest (v. 2), the care (v. 1), the provision (vv. 5-6), and the protection (v. 4) the shepherd provides betrays his deep knowledge of who the sheep are and exactly what they need in a given moment.

We see this elsewhere in scripture. The importance of "knowing" is reflected in Jesus' statement, "I am the good shepherd; I know my sheep and my sheep know me." An underdog church-planter cannot care well for his people if he does not know them, and likewise, if they do not know him. To start, this means the people of the congregation, the flock, must be identified. The church-planter must also know the flock personally, meaning that a personal relationship is established and growing with each "sheep". Practically, a single church-planter cannot do this with every person in a church over a certain size. These churches must develop intentional strategies so that a church leader is identified as a shepherd over every family or individual within the church body. The responsibility of knowing the sheep is particularly important when crisis situations and counseling needs arise.

Feeding the Sheep

Second, in verses 2, 5, and 6 of this psalm, we see God's desire to provide for the sheep. To paraphrase verse 1, "because the Lord is my shepherd, I am content and I want for nothing." He leads them to fresh water and provides for them an abundance of food. Likewise, in John 21, we see Jesus command Peter to "feed my lambs." This feeding is not, obviously, literal food. In Jesus' words, "People do not live on bread alone, but on every word that comes from the mouth of God." (Matt. 4:4)

For the underdog church-planter, the most obvious act of feeding the sheep is the weekly preaching of the Word of God. But more than that, feeding happens in community groups, Bible studies, discipleship groups, one-on-one counseling, etc. Feeding the flock is absolutely crucial to its health and vitality, and therefore to the pastor's care for the sheep.

Leading the Sheep

Third, the Lord's role in leading the sheep is clear in this Psalm. We read in verse 2 that the he "leads me beside still waters," and in verse 3 that he "leads me in paths of righteousness." This leading is not domineering or self-serving; rather, it is characterized by servanthood. Sheep often don't know what they need, or where to go to get it. The Lord's desire is to lovingly lead the sheep to what is best.

The same is true for the underdog church-planter. He must be a servant-leader, leading the flock for their good and not in self-service. Furthermore, as Peter points out in his first epistle, in leading the flock the shepherd is to function as an example for the flock. He is to be the model disciple, so that he can say with Paul, "be imitators of me, as I am of Christ" (1 Cor. 15:1). This is another way in which the church-planter cares for God's people.

Protecting the Sheep

Looking finally to verse 4, we read, "Even though I walk through the valley of the shadow of death, I will fear no evil, for you are with me; your rod and your staff, they comfort me." This is a description of the shepherd's protection for the sheep. Out of great love for people, the Lord keeps watch to protect the sheep in ways they cannot do themselves.

Similarly, the underdog church-planter must be prepared to protect the church. Paul, in Acts, warns about "savage wolves" who will not spare the flock but will distort the truth. The church-planter must be prepared to protect the church from those who would lead the sheep to dangerous theological terrain. Also, with his knowledge of the individual sheep, he will serve to protect the people as they walk blindly into dangerous life situations that arise.

The American church has provided us with a variety of models for the role of the church-planter, and yet God's Word is clear. Above all, the Biblical church-planter must be a shepherd. As enticing as these other models may be, we must return to a biblical model of shepherding. When we do, only then will we be able to heed Paul's words to "Keep watch over… all the flock of which the Holy Spirit has made you overseers. Be shepherds of the church of God." May this be the work of all pastors whom God calls into the service of His church.

Until now, we have been primarily concerned with *what* a pastor ought to do, and so we've unpacked a Biblical model of the underdog church-planter as shepherd. Now, I want to spend a few moments going beyond the *what* and looking at *how*. See, the risk in defining a clear (job) description of a Pastor-Shepherd is that it can be turned into a new profession, a set of rote activities for the self-disciplined person to simply check off. Indeed, certain churches have inherited a shepherding model, and yet they suffer under the leadership of a pastor doing the work without a shepherd's heart. And so, I want to consider five characteristics, heart qualities, of the biblical church-planter.

Characteristics of the Joyful Shepherd

Joyful

First and foremost, the underdog church-planter ought to have a joyful spirit. Scripture makes clear that the life of the Christian ought to be characterized by joy (Phil. 4:4), and the same is true for the church-planter. In Matthew 11, Jesus writes that all who follow his call will experience an easy burden and a light yoke; indeed, he offers rest for weary souls. John Piper's well known refrain is that, "God is most glorified in us when we are most satisfied in Him."[38]. This means not settling for self-willed drudgery but pursuing the promise of restful delight. Paul's exhortation to do all things to the glory of God demands that we do it joyfully. What a hopeful promise. The underdog church-planter is not called to serve out of duty but delight!

The Joyful Shepherd truly finds the work of shepherding a joyful work. Where others will find relationships tiring, the needs of the sheep overwhelming, and the pursuit of people burdensome, the Joyful Shepherd experiences fulfillment, for this is the work to which the Lord has called Him. He meets God in these moments and his call is realized. He does not "have to" deal with people, he gets to. While even the most joyful of shepherds will encounter times of discouragement, exhaustion, and difficulty, the broader experience of the joyful shepherd – the joyful underdog church-planter - is indeed one of joy.

Willing

Second, the Joyful Shepherd approaches the work of shepherding not under compulsion but willingly. This is Peter's qualification in his first epistle: "shepherd the flock of God that is among you… not under compulsion, but willingly" (1 Pet. 5:2). Similarly, when Paul writes to Timothy about the qualifications of elders, he tells us elders should aspire to this work (1 Tim 3:1). God does not desire that pastor-shepherds should care for the sheep begrudgingly, as if they were cleaning filth from bathrooms thinking, "well, somebody has to do it." On the contrary, God's under-shepherds should be eager to do this work—the King of Creation has gifted them for and called them to this!

When the phone call comes or the email is read, the joyful church-planter willingly serves the sheep. When a hospital visit is needed, the joyful church-planter doesn't dread the call, but is eager to care for this person in need. When a person stops by unexpectedly, the interruption—even though it is just that— is welcomed by this precious soul. The joyful church-planter knows his call is to selflessly serve the sheep, and he can do so because he's called by Jesus who selflessly served him first.

Pursuing

Third, the Joyful Shepherd is a pursuer of people. When taken as a whole, the story of scripture is the story of a missionary God who stops at nothing to redeem and restore His lost sheep. It's the story of a God who pursues people out of love, no matter how hard they fight, no matter how deep their brokenness. We see this as early as Genesis 3 when immediately after Adam and Eve's sin they hide from God and He pursues them, and likewise in the imagery of Revelation where He is standing at the door knocking (Rev. 3:20). Psalm 139 makes clear that God's pursuit is rooted in deep knowledge, care, and love for each of His precious sheep.

Jesus tells three parables in Luke 15 that further unpack the idea of God's pursuing love. God's care for each individual sheep drives Him to leave the herd of 99 and pursue the single lost sheep (Lk. 15:3-7). God's pursuing love is likened to a woman who lost a coin and stops at nothing to seek and find that coin (Lk. 15:8-10). God's love for His children is not deterred by their rebellion, and He is quick to lavish the repentant sinner with many blessings (Lk. 15:11-32). This sort of gracious, persistent pursuit is the precedent the underdog church-planter has been given.

The Joyful Shepherd, then, is called to pursue people because God first pursued us (1 Jn. 4:19). There are all sorts of reasons we come up with not to pursue someone: he was rude, she won't appreciate it, he won't respond anyway, she will take up too much of my time... and so on. And yet, what possible excuse could not every one of us be found guilty of before the Lord? Each of these things (rude, unappreciative, unresponsive, needy) and worse we have been toward God and yet His grace still abounds! And so our love must be driven onward for those in our churches. The joyful underdog church-planter is not content to hide in his study. He does not spend his week simply hoping and expecting people to show up on Sunday. He pursues the sheep because he greatly values the sheep, because *the Lord* greatly values the sheep and this pursuit is the work of the under-shepherd.

Humble

Fourth, the Joyful Shepherd is humble. It is important to note this may be the foundational quality, if not the most important, of any other characteristic of the underdog church-planter's heart. Listen to what scripture says about humility: "God opposes the proud, but gives grace to the humble" (Jas. 4:6).

"When pride comes, then comes disgrace, but with the humble is wisdom" (Prov. 11:2). "This is the one to whom I will look: he who is humble and contrite in spirit and trembles at my word" (Isa. 66:2). Jesus portrayed the deepest humility in taking on human flesh and dying an unrighteous death for sinners (Phil. 2:6-9). Make no mistake: God has no patience for the prideful man, much less the prideful church-planter.

In a world of false humility, where self-confidence and pride are the leading examples, the shepherd-leader knows he has nothing to prove. Christ has proven it all! The joyful church-planter has no need to live in fear of man because he lives in humility before God. The pastor can let go any pretense to have all the answers. He is not the best, the brightest, or the holiest of his church. He has simply been called by God to serve His beloved sheep.

Patient

Finally, the Joyful Shepherd is patient. Patience is one of the most gracious qualities of God seen throughout Scripture. God's very character is one of patience: "But you, O Lord, are a God merciful and gracious, slow to anger and abounding in steadfast love and faithfulness" (Psa. 86:15). "[He] is not slow to fulfill his promise as some count slowness, but is patient toward you, not wishing that any should perish, but that all should reach repentance" (2 Pet. 3:9). Indeed, Paul notes patience as the result of the Holy Spirit's work in a person (Gal 5:22).

For the underdog church-planter, the importance of patience cannot be underestimated. He is not fed up when things don't go his way, and he is not frustrated when his people don't see what he sees. When sheep fall into the same ruts and make poor decisions, he reacts not out of anger but gentle concern. To the extent that the Lord is long-suffering, the underdog church-planter is called to the same. He knows his success is not defined by speed of growth, but persevering faithfulness. God is sovereign and all things work out according to His timeline. The underdog church-planter's patience is a direct reflection of his trust in the Lord.

For Further Reflection

1. *How have you seen pastoral ministry modeled? Which of these examples would you like to carry on and which would you rather leave behind?*

2. *Which of the popular pastoral models do you find yourself most comfortably leading in? What are its benefits? How may this pose risks to your church?*

3. *Why do so many pastors avoid the work of shepherding? How is this justified by well-meaning, godly men?*

4. *Why does God choose to use a shepherd and sheep as a metaphor for Him and the Church, as well as a pastor and the local church? What implications does this have for your ministry?*

5. *Which characteristic of the Joyful Shepherd comes most naturally for you? Which do you most struggle with? How will knowing this affect how you lead?*

the underdog church-planter as...
courageous missionary

Dan Freng

"The gospel is only good news if it gets there in time."

- ***Carl F. H. Henry***

In late 1914, celebrated polar explorer Sir Ernest Shackleton, leader of the British Imperial Trans-Antarctic Expedition, set sail with a 27-man crew, bound for the South Pole in hopes of completely crossing Antarctica. Many of those who joined and were enlisted for the journey had responded to the following recruitment notice that Shackleton had printed in the London paper, *The Times:*

> "Men wanted for hazardous journey. Small wages. Bitter cold. Long months of complete darkness. Constant danger. Safe return doubtful. Honour and recognition in case of success."
> - Ernest Shackleton[39]

In response to his posted ad, Shackleton was overwhelmed with thousands of responses; men bravely wanting to take their chances on the icy voyage. Why in the world would anyone have signed up for this? A high-stakes, dangerous mission across uncharted waters, where you will make no money, spend most of your time freezing in the dark, and most likely not come back alive? Seriously, who reads an ad like that and goes, "This sounds like an awesome experience…I'm in!"? Someone with grit. Someone with guts. Someone with a stout-hearted willingness to give their life away to accomplish a mission. Someone with *courage.*

As underdog church-planters, we have been called by our Lord Jesus to join Him in a high-stakes, life or death mission. A mission to bring the life-giving, eternity-changing, joy-producing news of the gospel to people around the world, whose hearts are cold, dark, and dead in sin. Jesus has called us to join Him in His mission to extend His glory and expand His Kingdom. As we seek to carry out this mission, we have a real enemy, who is fighting against the extension of God's glory and the expansion of God's Kingdom at every turn. Our enemy is eager to kill, steal, and destroy the work of God and the people of God. This is no joke. This is no game. This great mission requires great courage.

As underdog church-planters, we live in towns and cities full of people who are far away from God and are ignoring Jesus. People all around us are searching everywhere to find purpose and meaning except the one place they will find it… in Jesus Christ. Our God has called us to join Him in His mission to save and redeem the broken and the lost. And He has called you, underdog church-planter, to gladly give your life away to pursue people who are running away from Jesus and tell them the great news that Jesus Christ came to earth to save them from their sins and to satisfy their souls.

The mission of every underdog church-planter is *to glorify God, by making joyful, passionate, disciple-making disciples of Jesus, in our cities and to the ends of the earth.* But, for us to courageously and faithfully carry out this mission, it is critical for us to understand, embrace, and surrender ourselves to the *motive*, the *Master*, the *method*, and the *means* for accomplishing our mission. We see all of these aspects of our mission in Matthew 28:16-20.

The Great Commission Defines and Drives Our Mission

Matthew 28:16-20, is a familiar passage for many of us as underdog church-planters. We have read it many times. We have probably memorized and memorialized it in our church vision and mission statements. But just because it is a familiar passage, doesn't mean we are always faithful to obey what it teaches. In these verses at the end of Matthew's Gospel, our Lord defines our mission and commands us to join Him in advancing His Kingdom and extending His glory. Church-planter, let me invite you to read these familiar words once again, but as you read them, pray for Jesus to humble your heart, sharpen your mind, and embolden your feet to follow Him more faithfully and courageously in His mission.

Now the eleven disciples went to Galilee, to the mountain to which Jesus had directed them. And when they saw him they worshiped him, but some doubted. And Jesus came and said to them, "All authority in heaven and on earth has been given to me. Go therefore and make disciples of all nations, baptizing them in the name of the Father and of the Son and of the Holy Spirit, teaching them to observe all that I have commanded you. And behold, I am with you always, to the end of the age. (Matthew 28:16-20)

The Motive of Our Mission: Worship

Before you go any further, ask the Lord right now to help you see the honest answers to few important questions: "Why do I do what I do as a church-planter?" "What drives me as a church-planter?" "What is my deepest motive for mission?" Be honest with God. Be honest with yourself. Is it the applause of others? Is it the feeling deep in your heart that you are okay because you talked to someone about Jesus today? Is it a desire to prove yourself to a parent, or spouse, or teacher, or former pastor? What is your deepest motive for mission?

Matthew 28:16-17 tells us that for Jesus' first disciples, the original underdog church-planters, the deep motive of their hearts, at the outset of their mission, was *worship*.

"Now the eleven disciples went to Galilee, to the mountain to which Jesus had directed them. And when they saw him they worshiped him, but some doubted." (Matthew 28:16-17)

Remember who these 11 guys were…ordinary, underwhelming, underdog guys. They were blue-collar, end-of-the-bench, last-to-be-picked, uneducated, unpopular, unprofessional dudes. Two things they all had in common: they were common, and because of the gracious of work of Jesus in their hearts, they passionately worshipped Jesus and were therefore radically committed to the mission of Jesus.

Don't miss this: our mission as underdog church-planters starts with worship; the glory, the fame, the non-ignorablity of Jesus, is our ultimate goal and purpose as missionaries and church-planters. Everything we do needs to start, persist, and end with our desire to "to glorify God, by making joyful passionate disciples of Jesus Christ." Notice what comes first in our mission – *to glorify God.* By God's grace, this must be our ultimate motive for everything we do in mission and ministry in our homes, on our streets, in our city, and in our world.

In *Let the Nations Be Glad!,* John Piper says this:

> Missions is not the ultimate goal of the church. Worship is. Missions exists because worship doesn't. Worship is ultimate, not missions, because God is ultimate, not man…Worship, therefore, is the fuel and goal of missions. It's the goal of missions because in missions we simply aim to bring the nations into the white-hot enjoyment of God's glory.…But worship is also the fuel of missions. Passion for God in worship precedes the offer of God in preaching. You cannot commend what you don't cherish…Missions begins and ends in worship.[40]

Church-planter, the driving force and the great goal of our mission is the enjoyment of the glory of God, both in our hearts, and in the hearts of those we seek to reach. As the Spirit leads us to humbly worship Jesus as our King, our King fills our hearts with humble courage to live on mission for His glory. The neighborhoods of our cities and the nations of the world are full of people who are not worshipping Jesus and are ignoring Him. God has sent us to make Jesus non-ignorable to them and pray for God to save them so that they might worship and enjoy Him now and forever more! Worship must be our greatest, deepest motive for our mission.

The Master of Our Mission: King Jesus.

So often as church-planters, we are tempted to believe the lie that we are the captains of our lives and in charge of the mission. Satan deceptively tempts us to believe the closing line of William Ernest Henley's poem, *Invictus:* "It matters not how strait the gate, How charged with punishments the scroll, I am the master of my fate, I am the captain of my soul."

But Matthew 28:18 reminds us that we are not the captain and we are not the master. The Captain and Master of our lives, and our mission, is Jesus. "And Jesus came and said to them, "All authority in heaven and on earth has been given to me" (Matt. 28:18). Make no mistake, when Jesus says, "all authority," He means *all authority.* That means there is no authority left for underdog church-planters like us to grab onto and try to leverage over the mission of our lives or the churches that we serve.

Jesus reminds us in this verse that He is not just some hot-shot leader, offering us a piece of helpful ministry coaching at a pastor's conference. He is

Jesus Christ – the King of the Universe – the Lord of all. The apostle Paul says this about our Master in Colossians 1:15-20:

> He is the image of the invisible God, the firstborn of all creation. For by him all things were created, in heaven and on earth, visible and invisible, whether thrones or dominions or rulers or authorities—all things were created through him and for him. And he is before all things, and in him all things hold together. And he is the head of the body, the church. He is the beginning, the firstborn from the dead, that in everything he might be preeminent. For in him all the fullness of God was pleased to dwell, and through him to reconcile to himself all things, whether on earth or in heaven, making peace by the blood of his cross.

Are you surrendered to Jesus as your Master? If so, then you need to daily embrace the reality that He has authoritatively sent you into mission. Jesus resolutely calls us to obey Him completely and that means joyfully obeying His command to give our lives away to make God's glory genuinely known, by making genuine disciples of Jesus. We are called by Jesus to a daily life of making disciples of Jesus… Not just vicariously making disciples through the ministry of people in our churches, but personally making disciples through a *real* commitment to introduce *real* people to the *real* Jesus, who has commanded us to make *real* disciples for His glory. Jesus is our Master and our Master has commanded us to join Him in His mission.

The Method for Our Mission: Go and Make Disciples of All Nations

In verse 19, Jesus gives us the fundamental method of our mission:

> Go therefore and make disciples of all nations, baptizing them in the name of the Father and of the Son and of the Holy Spirit, teaching them to observe all that I have commanded you. (Matt. 28:19)

Very simply, as underdog church-planters, our mission is to make disciples of Jesus. In his book, *Discipling,* Mark Dever says this about our mission:

> We follow the one who calls people to follow by calling people to follow. Why do we do this? For the sake of love and obedience. The motive for discipling

others begins in the love of God and nothing less…God's love for us starts a chain reaction. He loves us, then we love him, then we love others…Discipling others – doing deliberate spiritual good to help them follow Christ – demonstrates love for God and others as well as anything. But tied to our love is our obedience. Jesus taught, "If you love me, you will keep my commandments" (John 14:15). And what has he commanded? "Go therefore and make disciples of all nations, baptizing them in the name of the Father and of the Son and of the Holy Spirit, teaching them to obey everything I have commanded you. And behold, I am with you always, to the end of the age" (Matthew 28:19-20). Part of our obedience is leading others to obedience.[41]

Our mission, which has been commanded by Jesus, is to make disciples of Jesus. But, what exactly is a disciple? Very simply, a disciple is a student or an apprentice. In Jesus' day, a disciple was a student or an apprentice of a Rabbi, or teacher. Disciples would follow their Rabbi everywhere he went, learning from the rabbi's teaching, being trained to do what the Rabbi did, and over time imitating and becoming a lot more like the Rabbi. So, being a disciple of Jesus means following Him, learning from Him, imitating Him, carrying out His ministry and mission, and becoming increasingly like Him in the process.

As underdog church-planters, our mission isn't to simply make converts, people who just pray an empty prayer or raise their hands or walk an aisle. No, our mission is to make disciples – joyful, passionate disciples of Jesus – who love Jesus, obey Jesus, and over time, become more and more like Jesus for God's glory and their joy.

But how do we personally make disciples? Jesus gives us four simple action steps in Matthew 28:19: *make disciples, mark disciples, mature disciples,* and *multiply disciples.*

1. Make disciples of Jesus, by going to people who don't know Jesus, introducing them to Him, and pleading with them to turn from their sins and trust Him in faith.

Our daily mission to make disciples, begins with us pursuing people who don't know or love Jesus, with genuine love and genuine friendship. This means we take the initiative to identify people on our street or in our apartment buildings, who are not worshipping Jesus, and then seek to bless them and serve them in a genuine relationship. We go to them…we don't wait for them to come to us, and then we love them. We get to know them. We seek to serve them. This means starting friendly conversations with neighbors who are out doing yard work on a Saturday, or waiting to pick up their kids after school, or standing next to us in the grocery line.

After we take initiative and start new relationships, we then seek to spend time with people and cultivate a real friendship with them. This means we listen to their story and we get to know them as we ask good questions and seek to understand who they are personally and where they are spiritually.

But our mission doesn't end with listening. As we listen to them and learn their stories, with humble courage, grace, and truth, we need to boldly tell them the truth about who Jesus really is and what He has really done through His life, death, and resurrection to provide the only way for us to be rescued from God's wrath and welcomed into God's family. This means we need to tell them the truth about God and His glory, about our sin and its consequences, about Jesus and His saving work, and about our need to honestly take responsibility for our sins and to humbly turn from our sins and put our trust in Jesus. As we plead with them to turn from their sins and trust in Jesus, we must pray like crazy for God to save them.

2. Mark disciples of Jesus, by baptizing them in the name of the Father, Son, and Holy Spirit.

After God does what only He can do to save those that we're ministering to, we need to lovingly encourage and shepherd these new disciples towards publically declaring their identification with Jesus through baptism in a local church. Baptism is both a symbolic marking point of God's saving work in them and of their all-in commitment to Jesus. Baptism is a time for new disciples to say to the world, "By His grace, the Father has welcomed me into His family. Jesus has washed away my sins, rescued me from death, and by the power of the Holy Spirit, I have been raised to new life. I'm all in with Jesus. I have surrendered my life to Him and I am committed to following Him. He has given me a new name and I am now a part of His family and will live in community and on mission with this local church." As we make disciples, we need to lovingly lead them to follow our Lord's command to be baptized and marked as new disciples *"in the name of the Father and of the Son and of the Holy Spirit."*

3. Mature disciples of Jesus, by teaching them to obey everything Jesus has commanded.

Jesus instructed His disciples to obey His commands. In John 14, Jesus links our love for Him with our obedience to Him: *"If you love me, you will keep my commandments…Whoever has my commandments and keeps them, he it is who loves me."* (John 14:15, 21) Teaching new disciples to obey all that Jesus has commanded them is as simple as reading the Bible with them and then asking and answering two simple questions: 1. What is Jesus teaching us in this passage? 2. How can I obey Him in every part of my life?

Our mission requires that we spend time with people reading God's Word and helping them walk in obedience to the teaching of God's Word. This means the easy commands and the hard commands; not just when it is comfortable, convenient, or cool. Jesus commands His disciples to obey His commands completely and our mission to make disciples of Jesus requires us to help people mature as disciples of Jesus, by obeying the commands of Jesus.

4. Multiply disciples of Jesus, by making disciples in our neighborhoods and in all nations.

As church-planters, Jesus has sent us to make disciples in our neighborhoods and in every nation on earth. So we need to be willing to go across the street and across the world to make disciples. Right now, Jesus is calling and wants to send some of us across the world to make disciples in places where He is not yet known or named.

Church-planter, pray this prayer: *"Jesus, do you want me to follow your call to make you non-ignorable to unreached, underserved people and places around the world? If so, please give me the courage and the strength to go where you are not yet known or named and make Your name non-ignorably famous as I seek to make, mark, mature, and multiply disciples."*

God has sent us to make disciples of all nations, in our cities and around the world. Where is He sending you? To whom is He sending you? Why aren't you going? When are you going to go? Our mission as underdog church-planters is to glorify God, by making, marking, maturing, and multiplying disciples of Jesus.

The Means By Which Our Mission Will One Day Be Accomplished: The Power and Presence of Jesus With Us.

Matthew 28:20 gives us incredible hope and courage for our mission. "And surely I am with you always, to the very end of the age" (Matt. 28:20). As church-planters, we don't engage in this mission by ourselves, in our own strength, and through our own power. Let this fill your heart with courage-growing hope: God is for us, the Holy Spirit is in us, and King Jesus is with us, now and all the way to the end of the mission. His power and authority as the King of the Universe gives us hope because He can and will save people from their sin and change them to be more and more like Him. His compassion for sinners and commitment to saving people who are far away from Him gives us courage for the mission. We are reminded that He loves the people we are trying to reach infinitely more than we ever will.

Brothers, we don't make disciples of in our own strength. We carry out this mission by the power of the Holy Spirit within us. As church-planters, we've been sent by Jesus, to share the good news of Jesus, by the power and strength of Jesus, for the glory and honor of Jesus. Our responsibility as underdog church-planters is to be faithful in personally living as a missionary and to faithfully making disciples where God plants us.

Here is the question: Are we willing to play our part in God's rescue mission? Are we willing to do whatever it takes to reach the lost in our cities? Will we introduce kids, teenagers, seniors, men, women, and people who don't look like us, talk like us, or live like us to Jesus? Are we willing to do whatever it takes to spread the good news of our great Savior Jesus, even if it means a painful sacrifice of our time, energy, resources, and reputation to share the Good News of Jesus with those who don't know Christ?

This is our mission and eternity is at stake. This isn't simply a matter of getting people to join our club, or expanding our platform on social media. This isn't a game. This is about life and death, darkness and light, heaven and hell, the glory of God and the good of people. The stakes couldn't be higher, but the joy doesn't get any bigger! So, underdog church-planter, let's do this! Let's joyfully give our lives away to glorify God, by making joyful, passionate, disciples of Jesus in our cities and to the end of the earth!

For Further Reflection

1. What things get in the way or keep you from personally living on mission to "glorify God, by making joyful, passionate disciples of Jesus?"

2. Who are you personally discipling right now? If you are not personally discipling anyone, ask God to show you who He wants you discipling.

3. What other "missions" are you tempted to prioritize over the Great Commission?

4. How does Jesus' promise to be "with you always, to the very end of the age" give you courage to begin and continue making disciples?

the underdog church-planter as...
faithful preacher

Mark Hallock

"The work of preaching is the highest and greatest and most glorious calling to which anyone can ever be called."

- D. Martyn Lloyd-Jones

Perhaps more than at any other time in history, the Church of Jesus Christ is in desperate need of church-planters who faithfully preach and teach the Word of God. Not church-planters who entertain. Not church-planters who share original, interesting ideas about life. The Church needs preachers... Preachers who faithfully preach and teach the Word of God, for the salvation of the lost and the edification of the found. This is a primary calling of the underdog church-planter.

John Stott was right when he wrote, "Preaching is indispensable to Christianity. Without preaching a necessary part of its authenticity has been lost. For Christianity is, in its very essence, a religion of the Word of God."[42] Moreover, Stott nails it when he says,

> No attempt to understand Christianity can succeed which overlooks or denies the truth that the living God has taken the initiative to reveal himself savingly to fallen humanity; or that his self-revelation has been given by the most straightforward means of communication known to us, namely by a word and words; or that he calls upon those who have heard his Word to speak it to others.[43]

Sadly, in far too many circles, the very Word of God is failing to be preached in a way that is biblically or historically faithful to the type of proclamation that has marked the evangelical church for much of its history.

111

This is tragic. It is for this reason that it is so vital for underdog church-planters to grow in both conviction of, and practice of, faithful, biblical preaching. So the question is, "What exactly does faithful preaching look like? What are the marks of faithful preaching? What are the benefits of faithful preaching?" Before addressing questions such as these, it is critical that we begin in the right place and with the right posture.

Faithful Preaching begins with a Humble Posture before the Word

God is a God who speaks. He has spoken and his words have been captured and written down in the Bible for the sake of his people and his ultimate glory. This is critical for the understanding and practice of faithful preaching. We are called to preach the very words of God. In fact, Underdog Church-Planters are called to preach the words of God, and nothing else. As Haddon Robinson notes, "When a preacher fails to preach the Scriptures, he abandons his authority. He confronts his hearers no longer with a word from God but only with another word from men."[44]

Practically speaking then, preaching must always be saturated in God's inspired, inerrant, authoritative and sufficient written revelation as contained in both the Old and the New Testaments. And so, our growing conviction as ministers of the Word must be, "Preaching is not the business of speculating about God's nature, will, or ways, but is bearing witness to what God has spoken concerning himself. Preaching does not consist of speculation but of exposition."[45] Of course, this approach to preaching is not rooted in the preacher's arrogant claim to have discovered worldly wisdom or to have penetrated the secrets of the universe. To the contrary, the preacher dares to humbly proclaim truth on the basis of God's sovereign self-disclosure. God has spoken, and he has commanded us to speak of him and for him from His perfect word.[46]

When the underdog church-planter is rooted in this conviction of Scripture as God's Word, his aim will be to stand under Scripture, not over it. This is the posture of humility in preaching. And humility must be a defining mark of the underdog church-planter. God's Word rules over our preaching. The pulpit is His, not ours. It is not the role or responsibility of the preacher to speak his own thoughts, but God's thoughts.

Faithful Preaching is driven by a Humble Commitment to Biblical Exposition

If we are to speak God's thoughts and not our thoughts, then Scripture alone must be the foundation and focus of all of our preaching. It must shape and direct the content, shape, and delivery of our sermons. It is for this reason that Underdog Church-Planters must be committed to the discipline and practice of what historically is known as expositional preaching. What exactly is expositional preaching? Simply put, expositional preaching is that type of preaching which takes for the point of the sermon the point of a particular passage of Scripture. A sermon is expositional if its "content and intent are *controlled* by the content and intent of a particular passage of Scripture. The preacher says what the passage says, and he intends for his sermon to accomplish in his listeners exactly what God is seeking to accomplish through the chosen passage of his Word."[47] It is preaching in such a way that "the meaning of the Bible passage is presented entirely and exactly as it was intended by God...it is the proclamation of the truth of God as mediated through the preacher."[48]

Expositional preaching is desperately needed today. It is expositional preaching that will feed God's people with good, rich food week in and week out. It is expositional preaching that will not only help men and women mature in their love for God and people, but will also help prepare them to deal with the challenges and trials of life in a God-honoring and hopeful manner. It is expositional preaching that the Spirit will use to open the eyes of the spiritually blind and regenerate the hearts of the spiritually dead. It is expositional preaching that will serve as a rock solid foundation for a church plant as the lost are reached and disciples are made God's way for God's glory.

The benefits of expositional preaching for both the church-planter and the church plant are many. Let me briefly share four of them.

Benefit #1: Expositional preaching forces the preacher to be a student of God's Word.

Alistair Begg observes that after seminary, serving in their first church or church plant, pastors study to produce a variety of sermons for their people. But some, having preached them all, then move on to give another congregation the benefit of their study.[49] By contrast, whether serving an established congregation or a new church plant, "when a pastor is committed to the systematic and consecutive exposition of Scripture, he will never come to an end of his task. If we are not learning, we are not growing; and if we are stuck, we can be certain that our people will be stuck with us."[50] As a result, it is absolutely vital to keep coming to the Scriptures "in the spirit of discovery. We must learn to look for the surprises in the passage. We should not assume that we understand just because we have spent time in this passage before."[51]

The Scripture must first take root in the heart of the preacher and do a mighty work inside of him before he ever enters the pulpit. Unless preachers have been transformed by the text they are preaching, exposition will fail to have the life changing power that it should have. As the great Puritan theologian and preacher, John Owen, states,

> a man only preaches a sermon well to others if he has first preached it to himself. If he does not thrive on the food he prepares, he will not be skilled at making it appetizing for others. If the word does not dwell in power in us, it will not pass in power from us.[52]

Benefit #2: Expositional preaching forces preachers to deal with and teach the whole counsel of God for the edification and growth of the flock.

It is not a stretch to say that biblical literacy in the evangelical church in the United States is at an all-time low. This can make the job of shepherding God's people very difficult in this day and age. This is all the more reason why expositional preaching week in and week out is critical to feed the sheep well. Sadly, the reality is that not only do most of our congregants have an insufficient knowledge of the Scriptures, but many seminarians today are just as ill-equipped. Jim Shaddix observes how this scenario "leaves the preacher with two options: either resign to the generation by minimizing the role of the Bible in his preaching or determine to change the generation by systematically teaching the Scriptures. Systematic exposition, especially, enhances knowledge of the Bible. By careful, exegetical study through books of the Bible you will become a master of the Scriptures, and your listeners will become knowledgeable students."[53]

Benefit #3: Expositional preaching provides needed accountability to the preacher and his pulpit ministry.

Here are two primary ways in which expositional preaching helps to bring about needed accountability to the preacher. First of all, expositional preaching holds the preacher accountable to be faithful in proclaiming what God says in his word and not what the preacher simply *wants to say*. Shepherd-preachers are called to be faithful to preach all of Scripture and not avoid difficult passages in order to appease the congregation. A congregation must be fed the whole of the Bible, being exposed to difficult passages as well as the favorite passages of a preacher. This assures that the preacher will study and teach both difficult and easier to understand passages with needed pastoral precision and insight. Secondly, expositional preaching holds the preacher accountable to work hard in his study throughout the week. As opposed to other forms of preaching methodology, expositional preaching takes much time, thought, study, and prayer every week. This is good for the preacher, as well as for the congregation.

Benefit #4: Expositional preaching provides protection both to the congregation and the preacher of God's Word.

For example, expositional preaching helps to guard against using the Bible as a weapon to bring pain and hurt. Jim Shaddix puts it this way,

> sheep are known to be less than prim, proper, and brilliant animals. Shepherding these creatures will periodically give rise to the temptation to find a Scripture to rebuke in airing one in the public arena. Clearly, that is not a proper approach to preaching God's word. Consecutive, expositional preaching its truths guards against that temptation. The expository method allows the word of God, rather than our own inclinations, to speak to the current situation. As you faithfully proclaim the word of God, the Holy Spirit will apply the truths to your listeners.[54]

Faithful Preaching is saturated in a Humble, God-Centered Focus

God's ultimate goal is his glory. Therefore, the ultimate goal of preaching God's Word must be joyful and passionate worship of God, both for the preacher and for the listeners. True life change comes as a result of genuine heart change and true heart change comes as a result of worshipping and exulting in the Triune God. This is the one overriding theme in the Bible, which is seen from Genesis to Revelation: God has created all things for his glory. He has created the earth for his glory, the stars for his glory, the air for his glory, the mountains for his glory, the birds for his glory, and he has created human beings for his glory and his Church for his glory! All of this is to be celebrated and exulted in through God-centered, expositional preaching.

God is God-centered and his Word is God-centered. What follows must be the firm conviction and practice of expositional preaching that is God-centered. In the words of the Puritan pastor and theologian, Cotton Mather, "The great design and intention of the office of a Christian preacher is to restore the throne and dominion of God in the souls of men."[55]

Alistair Begg says, "Since expository preaching begins with the text of Scripture, it starts with God and is in itself an act of worship, for it is a declaration of the mighty acts of God. It establishes the focus of the people of God and his glory before any consideration of man and his need."[56]

A prime example of this type of preaching is the pulpit ministry of the great reformer, John Calvin. Calvin's preaching was doxological in nature, centered on God and his ultimate glory. As Nathan Bingham explains,

> All of Calvin's sermons were God-centered throughout, but his closing appeals were especially heartfelt and passionate. He simply could not step down from his pulpit without lifting up the Lord and urging his listeners to yield to His absolute supremacy. … As he concluded, Calvin regularly exhorted his congregation: 'Let us fall before the majesty of our great God.' Whatever his text, these fervent words called for the unconditional submission of his listeners.[57]

In light of his in-depth study of Calvin's God-centered, God-glorifying approach to the expositional proclamation of the Word, John Piper gives this powerful testimony of Calvin's lasting impact on preaching,

> God's word is mainly about the majesty of God and the glory of God. That is the main issue in ministry. And, even though the glory and majesty of God in his word can be known in the still small voice of whispered counsel by the bedside of a dying saint, there is something in it that cries out for expository exultation. This is why preaching will never die. And radical, pervasive God-centeredness will always create a hunger for preaching in God's people. If God is 'I Am who I Am' – the great, absolute, sovereign, mysterious, all-glorious God of majesty whom Calvin saw in Scripture, there will always be preaching, because the more this God is known and the more this God is central, the more we will feel that

he must not just be analyzed and explained, he must be acclaimed and heralded and magnified with expository exultation.[58]

One of the practical implications for Underdog Church-Planters of pursuing this kind of God-centeredness in the expositional preaching of God's Word, is the cultivation of humility and diminishment of self-centeredness that can so easily creep into the pulpit. Kevin DeYoung speaks to this temptation to make our preaching more about ourselves than about God and his Word when he writes,

> Permit me a brief word about a disconcerting trend I see in young, and sometimes very popular, preachers. I mention this concern knowing full well my own temptation to it. Let me pose the problem as a question:
>
> Preacher, are you at your best when you are closest to the text?
>
> Too many preachers are at their best when they are telling a personal anecdote or ripping into some sacred cow or riffing on in a humorous fashion. There is a time for all of that, but we ought to beware if those times are when we are at our best. We can be orthodox preachers of good, Gospel truths and still tickle people's ears. If we're not careful, we'll train the large conference audience and our local congregation that the time to really pay attention is when we start drifting not when we start digging.
>
> 'Got it. Understood. Text means this, not that. Sounds good. Now get back to that funny, over the top, in your face thing you do.'
>
> I've done that thing; probably will again. If the rant is honest and true, the Lord can use it. But, again, I repeat myself, it must not be the best we have. The congregation should be most aflame with Gospel zeal when they are beholding new things in the chapters and verses at the end of their noses. God uses all of the preacher–personality, humor, gestures–all of us. But the indelible impression left on our people must be a sense of the presence of God arising from careful attention to the word of God. If the best stuff we have every Sunday is disconnected from our hard won exegetical work, our people will learn to trust us and not the Book. They will look forward to our new antics, not our new discoveries in the text.

Ask yourself this Saturday: 'Can I make my best point–the one I'm most excited about, the one I can't wait to deliver–without noting anything from this week's passage?' Everything you want to say isn't everything you should say. We must be constrained by what we can sincerely say from these verses. If we want fresh power from the pulpit let us labor to demonstrate that our most passionate appeals come from the most precise exposition. The best preacher is the preacher who is at his best when he is closest to the text.[59]

Perhaps it is fair to assume there is not a single preacher who does not struggle with this area of pride. When you are "the man" who is leading and preaching, it becomes all too easy to fall into a people-pleasing mentality. A preacher can become hungry and needful of the affirming laughter when cracking a good joke or seeing the ripple of nods across the sanctuary when telling a relatable story. When not kept in check, the primary focus of God's glory and the proclamation of Scripture can all too easily take a back seat to pride, thus allowing self-centered preaching to become the norm.

Faithful Preaching is guarded by Three Humble Priorities
So, let's get very practical at this point. If Underdog Church-Planters are to have ministries marked by faithful, expositional, God-centered preaching of the Word, it is critical that they intentionally practice humility in their preaching week in and week out. The question is, "What exactly does this look like?" Though not exhaustive, let me suggest three essential, humble priorities for the faithful preacher.

Priority #1: The Focus of our preaching must always be Faithfulness, not Fame.

Being an "ordinary" pastor and preacher isn't the goal of many in our day. The rise of the "celebrity" preacher is alluring to many and consumes the hearts and minds of many a pastor in today's Church. The temptation to be known as "great" is prevalent in our star-struck evangelical culture. However, seeking "celebrity" is not the calling of the man God desires to preach his word and shepherd his flock. Indeed,

> God may need a few well-known preachers to broadcast the Word. But most of us are called to do the humble, faithful work of preaching in local congregations, small to middling, and to feed the flocks God has given us in those places.[60]

The bottom line is that God is honored in preachers that seek not to be good, "but to be faithful. The prayer for humility is a necessary one for those who proclaim God's Word.[61]

Any church that is built on the personality and gifting of the preacher is vulnerable to making that individual the hero, rather than Jesus. As Jared Wilson writes, "Your church needs to know that it is the Bible properly taught that is their source of strength, not a particular man and only that man teaching it. This is the inner error in many video venue enterprises. Some will say the satellite would not be viable without the "celebrity" preacher preaching, in which case I think it could be argued that if it could not survive without a particular person's voice, it is not viable to begin with. (What happens if that pastor has a heart attack? Does every satellite shut down? Or do they just play old videos?)." At the end of the day, we must do whatever it takes to assure that Jesus is made non-ignorable, not the preacher. The spotlight is His, not some pastor. Therefore, the focus must always be faithfulness, not fame.

Priority #2: The Preacher must always bring a Proper Fear of God into the Pulpit.

Perhaps the most foundational problem in so many pulpits today is a lack of the fear of God. For much contemporary preaching, there seems to be a lack of attitude and disposition in which one "regards the smile of God as his greatest delight, and hence his primary aim, and the frown of God as the greatest thing to be dreaded and avoided."[62] David Wells in his excellent book, *God in the Wasteland: The Reality of Truth in a World of Fading Dreams*, notes that "self has replaced God as central in preaching."[63] He rightly points out that, "God as holy and transcendent has been replaced by a God who is approachable, our buddy. The idea of personal holiness has given way to "psychological wholeness," and depravity has become a bad self-image or victimhood."[64]As a result, a lack of the fear of God has invaded the pulpit in many evangelical churches in our day. If we are to be faithful preachers of the Word, we must beg the Lord to constantly give us a proper, humble and healthy fear of Him and the weighty task of proclaiming His truth.

Priority #3: There Must be a Shared Commitment to a Team-Preaching Model.

One of the ways Underdog Church-Planters can intentionally pursue humility through their preaching ministry is by committing to a team-preaching model. In essence, a team preaching model is exactly what it sounds like. Instead of having just one pastor preach week in and week out, the pulpit is shared by a team of preachers. While the lead pastor may preach the majority of the time, in a team-preaching model, the pulpit is truly shared, as opposed to having a "guest" preacher show up once in awhile when the main preacher is gone. Let me share nine reasons why I believe this team-preaching approach is so vital to the health of a local church, along with how this approach has been so effective in the church where I pastor, Calvary Church-Englewood.

Reason #1: Obedience to Scripture. Calvary Church Englewood (along with all of our church plants) is led by a plurality of pastor-elders as taught in the New Testament. Not one. Multiple pastor-elders. The Scripture teaches that it is the responsibility of all the pastor-elders to preach and teach the Word of God to the flock, not just one individual (see Acts 6, 1 Tim. 3, Titus 1). This is a shared calling and responsibility. Sharing the pulpit in this way is about obedience to the Word and the way God wants His church to be led.

Reason #2: Setting the church up well for the future. A shared pulpit helps to assure that when the main preacher leaves or dies, the church remains steady and in a healthy spot to continue making disciples and planting churches. As leaders, we must be looking to the future. Our philosophy and practice of preaching *now* will radically affect how our churches look and function 5, 10, or 20 years from now.

Reason #3: Allows pastor-elders to eat (spiritually speaking)! One of the great joys and blessings in my own spiritual life is sitting in the pew and feasting on the preached Word as it is delivered by one of our other pastor-elders. I love seeing and hearing them preach to our congregation, but I also love being able to eat the Word they are preaching for my own soul. This is critical for the spiritual health of all of our pastor-elders.

Reason #4: Family leadership and discipleship. It's a joy to sit with my wife and kids and hear the Word of God preached, together as a family. As I feast myself, I also love the opportunity to help my family feast. Helping my kids learn how to listen to a sermon effectively is part of my calling as their father and spiritual leader. Along with our other pastor-elders, I am only able to do this in a shared preaching model.

Reason #5: Needed time for other pastoral duties. Weeks where I am not preaching allow me to spend more focused attention on other vital aspects to my ministry and leadership including pastoral care, vision and strategy, mentoring, preaching and teaching prep, denominational responsibilities, etc. As our church has grown, these important areas of ministry need more of my time and attention as the lead pastor.

Reason #6: Pacing for long-term leadership health. Any preacher will tell you, sermon prep is a joyful yet agonizing process. It takes incredible mental, emotional, spiritual, and physical energy every week. I typically spend around 20 hours a week preparing my sermons. Moreover, I preach hard for 40-45 minutes at three different services on a weekend. Over time, this will take a toll on a preacher if there is not a shared preaching model in place. I hope, by God's grace, to pastor and lead at Calvary for many years to come. If this is to happen, I cannot crush myself by not sharing the pulpit with other pastor-elders. No one can do this alone for the long-term in a healthy way.

Reason #7: The blessing of hearing a variety of unified voices in the pulpit. A shared pulpit allows our congregation to be fed by different pastor-elders, each with unique personalities and giftings. There is not one preacher who will connect with everyone in the same way in the same congregation. A shared preaching model helps our congregation to value and experience a variety of preachers, all committed to loving and shepherding God's people through the faithful, expositional preaching of God's Word.

Reason #8: Helping pastor-elders grow as preachers. As with all members of our church body, we must intentionally seek to equip and develop pastor-elders in using their gifts, specifically in the area of preaching and teaching. The last thing I (or our congregation for that matter) want to be complicit in is wasting the God-given preaching and teaching gifts of our pastor-elders.

Reason #9: It stirs up in me (and our other preachers) fresh passion and joy to preach. I have found that sharing the pulpit allows the Holy Spirit to refresh my heart and my mind on weeks I am not preaching. When I have a week or two off from preaching, I have time to remember why this calling to preach is so important and what a joy and privilege it is to feed God's people from His Word! This always spurs me on toward renewed zeal, joy, and excitement to get back in the pulpit and swing for the fences for God's glory and the good of His people!

Closing Words for the Faithful Preacher...

Healthy, growing churches are marked by the faithful preaching of God's Word. This has always been the case and it always will be. The Lord grows His Church, He matures His Church, He instills passion and zeal in His Church through faithful preaching. By God's grace, may the underdog church-planter seek to be God-centered preachers, humbly and joyfully surrendered to His perfect, authoritative Word. May the Spirit continue to fill us with fresh conviction and desire to feed God's sheep with good food that only comes from Scripture. Our lost world doesn't simply need more churches and church-planters. Our lost world needs more Underdog Church-Planters who will seek not to be "cool" in the eyes of the world, but faithful in the eyes of God through the exposition of His Word. Underdog Church-Planters are faithful preachers.

For Further Reflection

1. *How important is preaching to the health and growth of a church plant? Share some reasons in support of your answer.*

2. *There are many ideas and opinions on what preaching is and what it should look like in the church today. What are some of the key characteristics of faithful, biblical preaching?*

3. *Why is humility so important in the preparation and delivery of our sermons? What does humility look like in this process?*

4. *What does it mean to be God-centered in your preaching? What might this look like on a practical, week to week level? What kind of church culture does this kind of preaching produce over time?*

5. *What are some of the positives and negatives about a team preaching model? What are some steps you need to begin taking right now to begin implementing this kind of team preaching model in your church plant?*

the underdog church-planter as...
persevering pastor

Kevin Hasenack

"By perseverance the snail reached the ark."
- **Charles Spurgeon**

When I was asked to help with the project, I couldn't have been more excited! One of the things I love about being part of Calvary is how we work together to build up and train others for ministry. I love sharing my mistakes, my shortcomings, my major "I can't believe he did that" stories so that others can learn from my pitfalls, and in many ways, have a head start in ministry. There's no better way to do that than help with this project, right?

Then came my assignment for this project. "The Underdog Church-Planter as Persevering Pastor"... my heart sank. How in the world am I equipped to talk about perseverance in ministry when I have only been the lead pastor for a couple of months? How can a guy with such little ministry experience speak to perseverance and endurance in church planting?

What Does It Mean to Be a Persevering Pastor?

First of all, I want to define perseverance. A quick peruse though the dictionary sitting on my desk says perseverance is defined as, "the quality that allows someone to continue trying to do something even though it is difficult."[65]

I also want to define endurance. Why? Well, because to have perseverance, I'm suggesting that you must have endurance. So, flipping back a couple pages in my desk dictionary I found this: "the ability to do something difficult for a long time; the ability to deal with pain or suffering that continues for a long time; the quality of continuing for a long time."[66]

Now that we have those working secular definitions, what about framing those in light of a biblical worldview? What does the bible say about perseverance and endurance?

As we study God's word, we are confronted with the idea of perseverance over and over. Certain passages jump off the page at us when it comes to perseverance and endurance. One that I go to often is Romans 5:1-5:

> Therefore, since we have been justified by faith, we have peace with God through our Lord Jesus Christ. Through him we have also obtained access by faith into this grace in which we stand, and we rejoice in hope of the glory of God. Not only that, but we rejoice in our sufferings, knowing that suffering produces endurance, and endurance produces character, and character produces hope, and hope does not put us to shame, because God's love has been poured into our hearts through the Holy Spirit who has been given to us.

Where does that endurance come from? Does it come from just gritting our teeth and putting our heads down until we are on the other side of a tough situation? No! That endurance comes in and through God's love given to us through the Holy Spirit. That's the beauty of all of this, we can trust on God for perseverance and endurance in ministry. He has the plans laid out for us, we just need to execute the plan.

I had a plan for where this chapter was going to go and I was ready to grind it out. Then, like so many times in my life, God changed the trajectory. I was a week out from the deadline and I got a call from my dad in New Mexico. He called me with panic in his voice. "Son, I came home to find your Mom in the garage unresponsive. I'm scared…you need to come home."

I got back to New Mexico as soon as could. In what can only be explained as a miracle and perhaps one of the biggest evidences of God's grace I've ever seen, my mom survived. When I got to the hospital, she was in ICU and the outcome looked bleak. She was alive, but the road ahead was uncertain and was going to take a bit of time. Over the next couple of weeks I was in a role reversal. I wasn't the one being cared for, I was taking care of my mom and dad. Through the whole process, I was reminded by those close to me that trials and sufferings are given to us by God and we are to face them with joy. I know that, and I pray you do too. Yet, it seems as though God has given me plenty of chances to get it right.

You see, this latest situation with my mom was just one of many in the past couple of years in which I have had some significant trials in my life. I looked back though my journal I keep when I do my daily time with God and was reminded of some of the more difficult ones.

This first entry was early on in ministry. My wife, Jenn, and I had just arrived on the missions field in North Africa one month prior. At the time, we had been married just two short years, and wanted to do all that God had called us to, even when it seemed crazy. And the best word to describe those couple of years in North Africa is CRAZY...

God I know you have called Jenn and I to North Africa as missionaries, but if I'm honest I don't know if I can do this! We landed just over a month ago and as of today we are halfway though our first Ramadan here. Hearing the call to prayer 5 times a day, 7 days a week is exhausting. I feel like I tried just about everything to meet people and become friends, but with such little Arabic I feel like a stammering two-year-old. At this point learning Arabic seems impossible! I don't want to be here, I'm ready to leave. Yet...I'm reminded of that quote from William Borden: 'Say NO to self, say YES to Jesus every time.' Help me listen and obey, help me persevere and have the endurance to stay.

September 15th, 2008

Jenn and I did stay, in fact we made it through three more Ramadans before coming back to Colorado. I look back and laugh at two things; First, I never got better at Arabic, and second, those were just the beginnings of God shaping me into what he wants me to be in the future.

This next entry was one of the toughest to revisit for me. Jenn and I had just entered our 7th year of marriage and had been living in Denver now for three years. I had just finished seminary, and all seemed to be going according to plan. We thought we knew what was coming next...

Well, that was one of the hardest days of my life. Jenn called me yesterday morning telling me that she felt awful. I came home to find her cold, clammy, and very much pregnant. Charlie's due date isn't for 6 more weeks so we thought our trip to the doctor would be fairly routine. This was not the case. We were sent here to St. Joe's downtown.

It didn't take long for us to quickly understand that Charlie was coming much sooner than we expected. In fact, as I sit down to write this, I am watching my daughter sleep in the NICU. It's hard to believe that just 24 hours ago, I was in the O.R. wondering if I was going to lose both my girls. I still don't understand why this is happening, but I know I heard from you God. It was like you where there in that cold, chaotic operating room speaking to me. I'll do my best to understand there is joy in spite of suffering. I need your help though. Help me see that joy in this time is in knowing you more. You are my hope. You are all that I need.

August 27th, 2013

At the time of this writing, my beautiful wife is doing great and our sweet daughter is about to celebrate her 3rd birthday! God has been so gracious to us over the last few years in our young family.

This last entry is the one that made me step back a bit. This entry is the lead up to why I am now the lead pastor of Calvary Denver…

Back in September of 2013, Jenn and I decided to come with the first church plant that Calvary ever sent. It has been an amazing learning experience and I couldn't have asked for a better couple of years. In fact, it has given me a sharpened focus on what you have called me to do, God. Over the last few months, it has been decided that we will be part of the team that plants again, except this time it's in our neighborhood! I'm so excited and at the same time out-of-my-mind scared. Scared, because today it seems that we won't have a lead planter. Our team seems to be disintegrating before it even starts. God, I've started this journey thinking I am meant to be that "number 2" guy, not a lead planter. I don't have multiple degrees, I don't have tons of ministry experience, and at this point, I feel like I can serve this new plant the best from the second chair. Yet, I am getting lots of guys telling me to pray about stepping into the lead role. God, you know my heart. You know I want to do everything you ask. You ring the bell and I want to answer. So help me; help me see and understand your will in this situation.

December 5th, 2014

By February of 2015, I was meeting with some of the Elders of our sending church (Calvary Littleton) and the Elders of Calvary Englewood, where my buddy Evan was a student pastor. You see, I wrestled with God for months on the decision to step into the lead role and be an underdog church-planter for Calvary Denver and knew that I needed a couple of things in place to make this work.

First thing I needed was the best guy ever to have in the foxhole of church planting: Evan. This guy is not only one of the smartest people I know, but he and I couldn't be more different. This is great because in all of my weaknesses he is able to make up for them. God in his grace, put this team together in the way he did for a reason… and that was so a church could be planted in a specific part of Denver, Colorado.

Second, I knew I had no idea what to do and was going to have to be totally and completely dependent on God for everything. I couldn't rely on past ministry experience because I had never been an underdog church-planter before. I couldn't point people to my pedigree because there wasn't any. I sure couldn't put trust in my intellect because that well was, and still is, quite dry! This meant only one thing: I would have to be okay with being a one-star, no-name, "normal" pastor that trusts in the Lord for everything.

What can we learn from the men that have gone before us?

My dad had told me that one of the best ways to learn is to study those that went before us. I never really appreciated that statement until recently. When I starting gathering resources and searching for what it meant to be a persevering pastor, I knew I left a least a couple of stones unturned.

Over the years, I have had the privilege of getting to know a handful of pastors who have been doing ministry, in some cases, longer than I have been alive. One of those men is Pastor Chuck McCullough. He was my childhood pastor and still is the lead pastor of White Rock Baptist Church in White Rock, New Mexico. In fact, at the time of this writing, WRBC just celebrated 30 years with Chuck as their pastor.

I found this incredibly encouraging, especially in hearing that the average stay of a pastor is no where near that long. In fact, "A recent research poll from Lifeway Research suggested the average pastor's tenure in a local church is 3.6 years"[67] Knowing this, I thought it was best to ask him what three things had helped him persevere in ministry and what might help me as an underdog church-planter. This is what he sent me:

1. The way we face Trials/Suffering will show if we will make it the distance in ministry.
2. We must stay connected to God. Without abiding in him, we don't stand a chance.
3. Without your wife, you won't make it to the end. She is the better part of you anyway.

Upon reading those three bits of advice, I had no choice but to evaluate my own life and ask some tough questions. Every time trials and suffering come my way, am I handling them the way that God intends? Will I be able to go the distance in ministry even through suffering? Am I fully and whole-heartedly connected to Christ? When I look at my family (my wife and kids) are they on board with where we are going? Will we all make it to the end or will I risk losing/damaging my family if I continue down this path?

How can we, in humility and dependence on God, become Persevering Pastors?

Here's the practical part… the "how to" section (When I'm reading a book, this is what a skip to first). I hope you're asking, "Kev, how can I become a persevering underdog church-planter?" Knowing that this isn't an exhaustive manual on all things church planting, here are some key ideas:

1. Understand that there will be trials; there will be suffering. God gives us these for our good and we are to have joy in the midst of suffering. Also know this though, "No amount of good theology is able to take the pain out of suffering. Too often we allow ourselves to believe that a robust view of God's sovereignty in all things means that when suffering comes it won't hurt. God's sovereignty doesn't take away the pain and evil that confronts us in our lives; it works them for our good."[68]

2. We must stay connected to Christ. We have to abide in him just like we are taught in John 15. To do that though takes discipline in both prayer, and the daily reading of God's word. Donald Whitney said it best, "Nothing contributes to the growth of spiritual heat and light more than the persevering practice of the Christian spiritual disciplines. The disciplines are the bellows and the iron poker—tools in God's hands though which he stokes and blows upon the eternal fire He Himself invites in His people."[69]

3. Your family must be on board with you! More specifically and importantly, your wife needs to be *all in*. In order to survive in church planting, revitalization, church replants, and frankly all types of ministry, you need to have a health, happy, thriving marriage. If you are looking for more resources, ask and you shall receive! Check out "Date Your Wife" by Justin Buzzard, "You and Me Forever" by Francis Chan, or "The Meaning of Marriage" by Tim Keller for starters.

4. Pray. Seriously. Pray, pray, pray. "Pray hard and pray often. Pray for conversions. Often we have not because we ask not. Whatever your thoughts are right now about being involved in and type of gospel work, put this book down and get on you knees before God Almighty. That's the very best and most important thing you can do."[70]

For Further Reflections

1. What do you do when the pressure is on?

2. Describe a time in your life that God has used your circumstances to teach you about perseverance.

3. How will you be prepared for suffering/trials in ministry?

4. Who will help you in being a persevering underdog church-planter?

notes

CHAPTER 1   God Loves to Use Underdogs…And He Always Has
(Al Barerra)

[1] M. Gladwell, *David and Goliath: Underdogs, Misfits, and The Art of Battling Giants* (New York: Little Brown, 2013), 6.

[2] Ibid, 6.

[3] Hebrews 6:10-11 (NIV)

[4] M. Gladwell, *David and Goliath: Underdogs, Misfits, and The Art of Battling Giants* (New York: Little Brown, 2013), 103-106.

[5] L.B. Cowman, *Streams in the Desert*, ed. J. Reimann(Grand Rapids: Zondervan, 1997), Day 9.

[6] R.D. Bergen, *2 Samuel, Vol. 7, The New American Commentary* (Nashville: B & H Publishing, 1996), 179.

CHAPTER 2   A Theology for Underdog Church-Planters
(Evan Skelton)

[7] Ian Provan, *1 and 2 Kings* (Peabody, Mass.: Hendrickson Publishers, Inc., 1995), 147.

[8] Ibid.

[9] Ibid.

[10] D.A. Carson, *Scandalous: The Cross and Resurrection of Jesus* (Wheaton, IL: Crossway, 2010), 36.

[11] Ron Classen and John Koessler, *No Little Places: The Untapped Potential of the Small-Town-Church* (Grand Rapids: Baker Publishing Group, 1996), 26.

[12] Ibid., 27.

[13] D.A. Carson, *The Cross and Christian Ministry: Leadership Lessons from 1 Corinthians* (Grand Rapids: Baker Books, 1993), 39.

[14] D.A. Carson, *Memoirs of an Ordinary Pastor* (Wheaton, IL: Crossway Books, 2008), 148.

CHAPTER 3   A Look at the First Underdog Church-Planters
(Matt Whitt)

[15] I. Howard Marshall and David Peterson, *The Theology of Acts* (Grand Rapids, MI: Wm. B.Eerdmans Publishing Co., 1998), 359.

[16] Joseph Tenney, "Self Promotion and Our Fear of Obscurity," *Desiringgod.org*, October 23, 2014, accessed August 1, 2016, http://www.desiringgod.org/articles/self-promotion-and-our-fear-of-obscurity.

CHAPTER 4   The Underdog Church-Planter as Dependent Disciple
(Jeff Jung)

[17] Os Guinness, "Church Growth—Success At What Price?", *Ligonier Ministries*, April 1, 1992, accessed September 15, 2016, http://www.ligonier.org/learn/articles/church-growthsuccess-at-what-price/.

[18] James R. Edwards, *Mark, The Pillar New Testament Commentary* (Grand Rapids, MI: Eerdmans Publishing Co. 2002), 280.

[19] David E. Garland, *Mark, The NIV Application Commentary* (Grand Rapids, MI: Zondervan Publishing House 1996), 361.

[20] Ibid.

[21] C. John Miller, *Saving Grace* (Greensboro, NC: New Growth Press 2014), 11.

CHAPTER 5   The Underdog Church-Planter as Loving Husband & Father
(Fabian Perea)

[22] Josh McDowell & Bob Hostetler, *Right from Wrong* (Dallas: Word Publishing, 1994), 96.

[23] Alexander Strauch, *Biblical Eldership: An Urgent Call to Restore Biblical Church Eldership* (Colorado Springs, CO: Roth and Louis Publishers, 1995), 16-31.

[24] Dino Senesi, "40 Questions to help you coach in deep water," *The Send Network Church Planting Blog*, March 2014, accessed September 15, 2016, https://www.namb.net/send-network-blog/40-questions-to-help-you-coach-in-deep-water.

[25] Phil Downer, *A Father's Reward* (Eugene, OR: Harvest House Publishers, 1988), 112-113.

CHAPTER 6   The Underdog Church-Planter as Persistent Prayer
(Mark Hallock)

[26] E.M. Bounds, *Power through Prayer* (Atlanta, GA: Trinity Press, 2012), 6.

CHAPTER 7   The Underdog Church-Planter as Humble Leader
(Jim Misloski)

[27] Philippians 3:10.

[28] Philippians 2:5-8.

[29] Isaiah 50:4-9.

[30] Luke 11:13.

[31] Isaiah 50:4.

[32] Henri J. M. Nouwen and Roel De Jong, *The Wounded Healer: Ministry in Contemporary Society*, 2nd ed. (New York, NY: Crown Publishing Group, 2010) 87-88.

[33] John 16:33

[34] James C. Collins, *Good to Great: Why Some Companies Make the Leap and Others Don't* (New York, NY: Harper Business, 2001).

[35] Jeanine Prime and Elizabeth Salib, "The Best Leaders Are Humble Leaders," *HBR.org*, May 12, 2014, Accessed July 25, 2016, https://hbr.org/2014/05/the-best-leaders-are-humble-leaders.

[36] Richard J. Krejcir, PhD, "Statistics on Pastors," *Into Thy Word*, 2007, Accessed August 11, 2016, http://www.intothyword.org/apps/articles/?articleid=36562.

CHAPTER 8   The Underdog Church-Planter as Joyful Shepherd
(Steve Anderson)

[37] For those unfamiliar with this language, these four functions are explained in great detail in, Timothy Z. Witmer, *The Shepherd Leader: Achieving Effective Shepherding in Your Church* (Phillipsburg: P&R, 2010).

[38] John Piper, *Desiring God: Meditations of a Christian Hedonist* (Colorado Springs: Multnomah, 2003), 288.

CHAPTER 9   The Underdog Church-Planter as Courageous Missionary
(Dan Freng)

[39] Doug Keeley and Tim Magwood, "The Shackleton Expedition," The Mark of a Leader, October 20, 2011, accessed August 1, 2016, http://www.themarkofaleader.com/the-shackleton-expedition.

[40] John Piper, *Let the Nations Be Glad!* (Grand Rapids: Baker Academic, 1993), 17.

[41] Mark Dever, *Discipling* (Wheaton, IL: Crossway, 2016), 16-17.

CHAPTER 10 The Underdog Church-Planter as Faithful Preacher
(Mark Hallock)

[42] John Stott, *Between Two Worlds: The Challenge of Preaching Today* (Grand Rapids: William B. Eerdmans Publishing Company, 1982), 15.

[43] Ibid.

[44] Haddon Robinson, *Biblical Preaching* (Grand Rapids, MI: Baker Academic, 2001), 18.

[45] R. Albert Mohler, *He Is Not Silent* (Chicago, IL: Moody Publishers, 2008), 41.

[46] Ibid.

[47] Mike Bullmore, "A Biblical Case for Expositional Preaching," *9Marks Journal* (May-June 2007), accessed June 5, 2013, http://www.9marks.org/journal/biblical-case-expositional-preaching.

[48] John MacArthur, "The Mandate of Biblical Inerrancy: Expository Preaching," in *Preaching: How to Preach Biblically,* ed. John MacArthur (Nashville, TN: Thomas Nelson Publishing, 2005), 18.

[49] Alistair Begg, *Preaching For God's Glory* (Wheaton, IL: Crossway Publishers, 1999), 34.

[50] Ibid.

[51] Ibid.

[52] Ibid.

[53] Jim Shaddix and Jerry Vines, *Power in the Pulpit: How to Prepare and Deliver Expository Sermons* (Chicago, IL: Moody Publishers, 1999), 34-35.

[54] Ibid, 35.

[55] John MacArthur, *First Timothy MacArthur New Testament Commentary* (Chicago, IL: Moody Publishers, 1995), 99.

[56] Begg, *Preaching For God's Glory*, 33.

[57] Nathan W. Bingham, "10 Distinguishing Marks of John Calvin's Preaching," *Ligonier Ministries,* August 16, 2013.

[58] Ibid.

[59] Kevin DeYoung, "The Preacher at His Best," *Gospel Coalition Blog,* accessed February 4, 2014, http://theGospelcoalition.org/blogs/kevindeyoung/2013/08/29/the-preacher-at-his-best/.

[60] Clayton J. Schmit, "Is There a Crisis in Preaching?,"accessed July 10, 2014, http://www.clayschmit.com/articles/Is%20There%20a%20Crisis%20in%20Preaching.pdf.

[61] Ibid.

[62] Al Martin, "What's Wrong With Preaching Today?" (sermon, Westminster Theological Seminary, Glenside, PA, September, 1967).

[63] David Wells, *God in the Wasteland: The Reality of Truth in a World of Fading Dreams* (Grand Rapids, MI: Eerdmans Publishing, 1995), 120.

[64] Ibid.

CHAPTER 11 The Underdog Church-Planter as Persevering Pastor
(Kevin Hasenack)

[65] *Merriam-Webster Dictionary, Vol. 1.,* Fredrick C. Mish, ed., 11th ed. (Springfield, MA: Merriam-Webster, 2009).

[66] Ibid.

[67] Dr. Franklin Dumond, "Eight Point Eight Two: How Long Do Pastors Stay in One Church?", *For Every Man,* June 26, 2014, accessed August 1, 2016, http://www.gbjournal.org/8-82/.

[68] John Piper and Justin Taylor, *Suffering and the Sovereignty of God* (Wheaton, IL: Crossway Books, 2006).

[69] Donald S. Whitney, *Ten Questions to Diagnose Your Spiritual Health* (Colorado Springs, CO: NavPress, 2001).

[70] Mez McConnell, *Church in Hard Places: How the Local Church Brings Life to the Poor and Needy* (Wheaton, IL: Crossway, 2016).

ACOMA PRESS

Acoma Press exists to make Jesus non-ignorable by equipping and encouraging churches through gospel-centered resources.

Toward this end, each purchase of an Acoma Press resource serves to catalyze disciple-making and to equip leaders in God's Church. In fact, a portion of your purchase goes directly to funding planting and replanting efforts in North America and beyond. To see more of our current resources, visit us at *acomapress.org*.

Thank you.

.

www.ingramcontent.com/pod-product-compliance
Lightning Source LLC
LaVergne TN
LVHW051743080426
835511LV00018B/3210